Swinging for Beginners
An introduction to the Lifestyle

Swinging for Beginners
An introduction to the Lifestyle

Kaye Bellemeade

New Tradition Books

Swinging for Beginners: An introduction to the Lifestyle
By
Kaye Bellemeade

New Tradition Books
ISBN 193242007X

For the swingers and for the wannabes.

Also for my husband. You have made my life a joy.

It's been said that the couple who plays together, stays together.

Contents

Swinging: What's it all about?

Swinging is all about having fun as a couple, first and foremost. It's is a way for a couple to expand their horizons by agreeing that sexual encounters outside (and inside) the relationship are permissible. It is a way for a couple to *be* a couple while allowing and accepting individual desires and needs. Couples who swing explore their sexuality and their fantasies. These couples can break the chains of jealousy and experience a more passionate and fulfilling relationship, as well as connecting on a deeper spiritual level. Swinging can give them the opportunity to grow as a couple *and as individuals.*

You might not realize it but swinging has been around for centuries. It's really nothing new, among us or other animals. An interesting story I heard recently was about an anthropological study dealing with monkeys. Apparently they don't always have sex purely for procreation. They do it to get off, as well.

The anthropologists watched these moneys for years and recorded their behavior. They noticed these monkeys were getting it on with other members of their tribe almost at whim. They would switch from one partner to another indiscriminately. And the ones who weren't having sex would stand back from the group and masturbate as they watched.

They were swinging. More to the point, these monkeys were having group sex.

While I am certainly not comparing swingers to monkeys, I think this study should let the rest of us know that swinging really isn't that big a deal. It's always been around and always will simply because people like to have sex with a variety of partners.

We are human and humans have basic desires. We need sleep, we need food, and we need sex. And, yes, I believe we need it. It's as basic a need as eating. Society tends to forget this. Personal human contact is essential. It makes you a better person to love and be loved. This feeling gives you courage.

Consider this: If you could have one meal everyday for the rest of your life what would it be? Steak? Tofu? Keep in mind it's only one meal but it can be *anything* you want.

A bit boring, isn't it?

This is why people swing. They can have their main meal anytime they want, everything they need is in that one meal, but every once in a while, they'd like to sample something different. It gives life flavor. It makes it more exciting. It adds spice.

Swinging helps ease the boredom of a long term relationship. After you experience swinging and get over your hang-ups, sex with your partner can be outstanding. You might want to do things with him/her you've never tried before. It might also make you feel good to see others enjoy what your partner has to offer. Knowing that they are yours and you get to go home with them is the best feeling. It really makes you appreciate what you have.

Swinging can make your relationship better. It can make it grow. You will find new reasons to stay with your partner and love them even more than you already do.

Keep this in mind: Like having a baby, swinging *will not* save a troubled relationship. In fact, it may break it apart. You must already have a strong bond in order to do it. It is not something to be taken lightly because it can and will change the nature of your relationship. It can make it better or it can make it worse.

To reiterate, swinging is *not* a ticket out of a bad relationship. It is not justification for cheating on your lover. And if you are using it as a last resort, it might blow up in your face. As I have said, swinging is a way for two people to connect on a deeper level. If you can look at the person you're with and truthfully say, *This is the person I want to spend the rest of my life with*, then swinging may be for you. It is as much a spiritual journey as it is about having good time. It is a bonding experience for a couple and a way to improve the quality of your existing life, not change it entirely. It is not a way to settle the score, nor is it a way to get even for past hurts.

This book is the nuts and bolts of swinging. I am an experienced swinger. I have been to the clubs, parties and dated many couples. However, I do not claim to be an expert. I am just an ordinary person who has been involved with swinging for several years. My intent when writing this book was to simply discuss what I know about non-traditional relationships, mainly focusing on swinging.

Please note I am *not* dispensing advice. I am only outlining my experiences and the experiences I have witnessed or been told by other swingers. This is in no way a self-help book. Take what you will but know that it is only applicable to my own personal experiences.

If this is something you want to do, I'm going to tell you how it's done and what to expect. I am giving you the knowledge I have and also my experiences, good *and* bad. I will also deal with the emotional aspects of swinging as they are a big part of swinging and are typically overlooked. Most people think it's all fun and games and that there is no emotional baggage. Be warned, there is a lot of emotional baggage, but once you get through it, it will well be worth it. However, *the decision to do it is entirely your own.*

And, this goes without saying, *the particulars of each story has been slightly changed and the names altered to protect the people who told them.*

You swing not because you want to fall in love with someone else. You swing to fall in love with your partner all over again. To see them in a new light, as the person they really are.

If you go into swinging with your mind and eyes open, you can experience what I like to call *true freedom.*

Why did you pick up this book?

Before we go any further, let's address this issue. Why did you pick this book up? Was it curiosity? Or was it because you really want to be a swinger? You might be looking for assurance that everything will turn out fine.

Many people want to be assured that going into swinging is the right decision. They want to be assured that if they go into it, everything will turn out okay. Am I right? Before I started swinging, I had these same thoughts. However, I didn't have anyone to assure me. It was a risk I had to take on my own.

If you want to swing, you are probably looking for an excuse to do it. There is really no excuse and you don't *need* an excuse. Wanting to explore one's sexuality is natural and doesn't have to be explained. On the other hand, if you're looking for an excuse *not* to do it, then it may be best that you don't.

The decision is yours and it's a tough one. Will this book help? I would like to think so, but in the end all I can really do is give you my personal experiences. Therefore I can't make your decision for you. This book can't either.

If you've been thinking about swinging for months or maybe even years, there is something about it that appeals to you. However, you have to have balls to swing. You cannot wait on other people to come to you. They won't. If you never put yourself out there, you'll never know what you're missing, if anything. You might find that it's really no big deal and you haven't missed out on anything at all.

The most important thing I can emphasize is that you need to be completely honest with yourself, first and foremost. Getting down to your real desires can be a tricky if not scary thing. It is my opinion that you don't really need justification for wanting to have sex with other people. And, other than your partner, you don't have to discuss this aspect of your life with anyone else. While I don't think it's anything to be ashamed of, this is probably the best course of action considering the way society views swinging. You may not have a problem with it, but be assured other people will. And it's none of their business.

#1 Rule of Swinging:

Swinging is what you make it. Swinging is about letting go of outdated notions about sex and relationships. It's about giving up hang-ups and allowing yourself to be completely free while allowing your lover to do the same.

Who are these so-called swingers?

There are numerous ways people view swingers. The actual term "swinger" gets thrown around a lot. Some think of swingers as a cartoonish Austin Powers or an elegant Hugh Hefner. Both of these images are somewhat inaccurate. Those images involve swinging men. Swinging *single* men. And you might want to know that most swinging single men are *nothing* like Austin Powers or Hugh Hefner. Unfortunately.

As far as couple swinging goes, some might think of swingers as older, less attractive people who are bordering on being perverted. This description is also inaccurate. There are countless younger couples in the Lifestyle and they're starting younger and younger.

But why would anyone want to be a swinger? The reasons vary from couple to couple but mostly it's about having sex with other people. People may have married too young and didn't get to "sow their wild oats". Maybe they were virgins when they married and have only experienced sex with their spouses. Maybe they have unrealized fantasies like threesomes or group sex. Maybe they just want more sexual variety by watching their lover having sex with another person. Maybe they really don't have a reason but know it is something they would like to explore because it just makes sense to do it.

Swinging, for some, may be the answer. Many couples deny that they want to have sex with other people and they divorce because of it. Of course, no one ever comes out and says it, but many times it's the real reason. We all have it in us to be sexually promiscuous. We all desire the touch of others. And, if denied, this desire can drive a person crazy. Therefore, swinging *may* be an alternative to divorce.

A male swinger friend once told me, "I know she wants to have sex with other people. I know I do, too. What's the big deal? We're people and people want that kind of thing. I'm just glad we can admit it to each other. Why divorce over it?"

Though sexuality is a huge part of a relationship, it is not all there is to it. Everyone knows that. Some couples don't want to split because of children. They might have a great house or own a business together. Most people don't want to split up over sex because it's a stupid thing to do.

But, of course, the most popular reason people don't want to split up is simply because they love one another.

An important thing to remember is that the people who swing are normal, everyday persons. The have regular jobs, they have families, many have children. The people I have encountered come from all walks of life. I've met doctors, MBA's, salespeople, people from the military, secretaries, teachers, business owners, pilots, soccer moms, minivan dads. From white collar to blue, from rich to middle class to working class, swinging extends across all social and economic borders and allows you to mingle with people in a way you never thought possible.

What is the age range? All ages, from early twenties to seventies. If you're younger, don't be intimated by the older swinger couples. I have found them to be the coolest people in the world. You can learn a lot from them. They are at that point in their lives where they no longer have the insecurity issues of younger people. They are what we aspire to be: free, open and cool.

It is my opinion that swingers don't care what you or anybody else thinks of them. They're too cool for that. They know that what they're doing—having sex with other consenting adults—might not be the norm, but it is the norm for them.

I have two mottos. The first: *Do as you please as long as you're not hurting anyone else.* And the second: *Don't knock it till you try it.*

How sexually adventurous are you?

How does the thought of having sex in a roomful of people sound to you? How does the thought of your *lover* having sex in a roomful of people make you feel? Does it make your stomach bottom out? Does it give you an excited, if nervous, feeling? Does it *appeal* to you?

Do you mind using the terminology? How do you feel about these terms: Fuck, cunt, suck, pussy, dildo, swinging? Do they make you blush? Or can you take it or leave it? Perhaps, it's a regular part of your vocabulary.

Swinging can be pretty hardcore and if you've never experienced it, it might make you a little uncomfortable at first. In fact, it should make you a little uncomfortable. However, if it makes you *extremely* uncomfortable or you find yourself passing judgment on people who use language like this or who do these kinds of things, it might be best that you not proceed. You will hear these terms at most swing parties and usually on dates. You will see lots of sexuality on display in all forms at clubs and parties.

Swingers are usually very down to earth people. This doesn't mean they're coarse because they use this type of language or do these things, it just means they're comfortable with their sexuality.

Ask yourself:

- Do I moan when I'm having sex?
- Do I enjoy sex?
- Do I like having the lights on when I'm having sex?
- Do I make passes at my lover on a regular basis?
- When I see other couples in public making out, does it excite me?
- Do I have regular or frequent sexual fantasies about other people?
- Do dirty talk and other fetishes interest me?
- Do I have sex other places besides the bed?

If you answered yes to most of these questions, you are definitely swinger material. If not, you might want to consider why you responded in the negative.

First of all, ask yourself why you want to be a swinger. Only once *you* are comfortable with it can you bring the subject up to your lover. Take a look at yourself first and don't be afraid to be completely honest. If you can't admit things to yourself, how can you admit them to others? Don't be afraid to do a little soul searching. Swinging is a journey and it starts with you.

Let's jump right in and start with a question you should ask yourself. *How does the thought of your lover kissing someone else make you feel?*

Note: *It should make you somewhat uneasy.* But *not* to the point of anger or devastation. If you see red, do not proceed. It is my opinion that you will not be able to handle it. So ask yourself this question and please be *COMPLETELY HONEST.* Honesty is paramount here. If you can't be honest with yourself, you can't be honest with your partner and you *have* to be honest with your partner. You have to come to terms with it. And it's a big step that won't be easy.

Once you get over hang-ups, the possibilities of what you can do and explore are endless. Things you were too uptight to try before suddenly seem like a good idea: Girl on girl, threesomes, group sex, getting naked in front of strangers, exhibitionism, interracial. All these things and many more become a possibility. In fact, they can become a reality.

But getting to that point can be a little tricky. Let me tell you how I got there.

Personal experience:

About four years into my marriage, I began to feel different. I don't know what happened, but one day I woke up and I just needed something more in my life, though I couldn't actually describe *what* I needed. It was like something was missing.

My partner and I had gotten married very young and we both had very limited previous sexual experience. Though we loved each other more than anything, I began to wonder what it would be like to have sex with men other than my husband.

At first, I was ashamed of my feelings. *How could I feel this way when I was with the love of my life? He takes such good care of me and loves me so much, I would be such a bitch to tell him how I really feel.* I didn't dare speak to anyone about my feelings because I was sure that I was the only one who had ever felt this way. I was sure everyone would judge me harshly because of it.

Well, it was enough to drive a person crazy. I fantasized about other men all the time. I was itching to have another man touch me. Yet, I could not bring myself to tell my husband. And if you think about it, (and have no knowledge of swinging) is it really a good idea to tell the one you love,

"Honey, I love you but I have to fuck other people. If I don't, I will go crazy and bring you along for the ride"?

So instead of being honest, I hid my feelings. Because of this, I began to get depressed and angry. I took a lot of my anger out on my husband. To this day, I am ashamed of some of the things I said and did. I made his and my life miserable because I could not tell him about my real desires.

The only solution I could see would be to fall out of love with him and divorce. That way, I wouldn't have to "justify" my feelings and I could have sex with other men. However, you can't just stop loving someone at the drop of a hat. I was very naïve to think this. I was also very stupid. I risked a very valuable relationship because I wanted to explore my sexuality.

Our marriage got very, very bad for a while. We stopped talking to each other, we stopped having fun, and we almost stopped loving one another. And sex? What was that? We went for weeks without sex. (This is unfathomable to me now.)

One day, during a fight, he asked me, "Why have I done? Just tell me what I have done."

I couldn't. Even when he asked, I couldn't. Besides, he hadn't done anything. It was all about me. It was about my desires and what I wanted to do. I felt that, in a way, he was keeping me from doing what I wanted to do. And that's why I picked fights with him. Maybe I was trying to make him leave so I could do what I wanted to do. Then if it all went wrong, I could blame it all on him.

It might be worth mentioning that I had been raised in a very strict household and was taught to think that sex was "bad" and "dirty" and "disgusting". I know my mother had told me these things to protect me from teen pregnancy, yet she did some major damage. While I absolutely loved sex and the way it made me feel, I could not reconcile my feelings after the deed was done. I felt bad afterwards and I was more than sure God would punish me for all the good feelings I had during sex.

So, therefore, how could I tell my husband I wanted to have sex with other people when I personally thought it was wrong?

This went on for about two years. By this time, we were both sick and tired of fighting and just about sick and tired of one another. I told him I wanted a divorce. He reluctantly agreed and I called a lawyer, got an appointment and we got into the car and were on our way when I burst into tears. I just started crying and I couldn't stop. I didn't want a divorce. I didn't want to be without him. But I couldn't give up these fantasies about sex with other people either. I couldn't "get rid" of my desires.

He asked me what was wrong and I said, "I don't know, but I don't want a divorce."

"Me either," he mumbled.

So we decided to call off the divorce. But I still didn't confess. I am very lucky to have such an understanding man. Surely, someone without his patience and understanding would have left me.

And the day came. It did finally come. A year or so later, we were drinking wine and listening to music when he said, "You really like this band, don't you?"

I nodded. I really liked the lead singer. He was one of my major fantasy guys.

He just studied me and blurted, "You want to fuck the lead singer, don't you?"

I was shocked. I was mortified. I was relieved.

I reluctantly told him, "Actually, yeah. I wouldn't mind it."

He nodded and said, "I kinda figured that."

So the cat was let out of the bag. *What if he was okay with the idea of me having sex with other people?* At first the thought terrified me. *What if he was? What if he wasn't?*

To be honest, I didn't know hardly anything about swinging nor did I know anyone who swung. In fact, I was pretty naïve and barely even knew it *existed.* I mean, I had heard of it but didn't think that people actually did it. I had no idea of what it was all about.

Then I started thinking that he thought I wasn't in love with him anymore. For some reason, I thought wanting to have sex with other people meant not being in love with your partner. (Sometimes I think I think too much.) But I was still in love with him. And I hoped he felt the same way.

I screwed up my courage and asked him, "So what do you think of that? I mean, me having sex with someone else?"

He stared at me, and then looked away. "Who says I don't want to do it, too?"

Well, there you go.

I couldn't think of anything to say. For a moment, I sat there and just let the enormity of what he was saying sink in. And depending on what I said and his reaction to what I said, the next words out of my mouth would change my world.

"How would you do something like that?" I asked.

He shrugged. "Haven't you ever heard of swinging?"

I had, but I didn't know that much about it. I had a lot of stupid, pre-conceived notions about swinging and the types of people who swung. Boy, was I in for a rude awakening. I would later find out that everything I knew was basically wrong. Much to my surprise and delight.

We talked a few more hours and decided we'd give a try.

He told me, "And if we don't like it, we can always stop. And we don't have to go crazy over it. It's just sex."

We decided, as a couple, that we needed to explore what was out there. Just not *knowing* is what spurred us on. We had married very young and though we had plenty of good years—and great sex—there were times when we were bored with each other. By taking a step to include swinging in our lives, we took a risk. Though in the end, it was well worth it, we didn't know how it would change our feelings. We didn't know if we would fall out of love or if we would meet other people we might want to be with. It was a risk for us as much as it is a risk to anyone who tries it. But not knowing, not exploring our sexuality was eating us both alive, though we didn't discuss it until that night. We were afraid to take that step. But it was one we had to take; otherwise we might not be together now.

We got lucky, though. We now have a deeper relationship. We know sex with other people is just sex. It's fun, it's great, but we know we go home together.

Related experience:

I've known Candy since I first started swinging.

"We almost divorced several times. I couldn't just come out and say to my husband, 'I want to have sex with other people.' It was just too hard for me. I couldn't face up to it myself, let alone tell someone else about it and that someone being the man who was 'supposed' to be everything to me. But people can't really be everything to each other. It isn't possible.

It was driving me crazy. I'd think about sex with other people all the time and I really wanted to explore my sexuality with other women as well. But I couldn't say it, let alone do it. I was just so inhibited.

I was a prude and I don't have a problem saying that. I wanted the lights out when we were having sex and I didn't like giving blowjobs. But there was something in me and I can't explain what it is, but that something was driving me crazy.

I guess it all changed when I started to lose weight. I was really overweight a few years ago and I took a good look at myself in the mirror and I thought, 'This isn't me.' I had been living someone else's life, the life I was 'supposed' to live. And it was tearing me up inside.

I started working out and eating better and the weight came off. My husband started to see me in a whole new light. I saw myself differently as well. I felt better and I felt sexier. I started to wear sexier clothes and felt more confident.

But my life was still not where I wanted it to be. I'd lost the weight because I wanted to appear sexier to other men (and women). I wanted to feel my sexuality and I wanted to flaunt it.

The decision to swing came about quite accidentally. My husband and I were driving by a strip club and I asked him if he ever wanted to go in one of those places. Well, that set the wheels in motion and the next thing I know, we were talking about being attracted to other people and then actually having sex with them.

I put it out there and he bit. Now we never even talk about divorce though it was a very real thing for us at one point. We even once had the papers drawn up. But I couldn't go through with it. I loved *him* and my desire for other people didn't have anything to do with him. Divorce may have been the quick fix but swinging was what saved us.

Actually, swinging might be secondary. Though it has allowed us to be freer and more sexual, I think just being able to *talk* about it and *knowing* he won't freak out when I fuck other people is what really counts. It makes me a whole person to know I can be who I want to be and be totally accepted for it.

And I don't have to hide from myself or anyone else anymore. I am the person I am. And I accepted that.

For me, it was a gradual change. It didn't happen overnight. I just knew there was something else out there and I wanted to get my hands on it. I have never regretted it at all."

I couldn't have said it better myself. *I have never regretted it at all.*

Check yourself.

If you are uncomfortable with the word *fucking* you are not swinger material.

Does this mean we're not in love anymore?

A lot of people make this assumption. Maybe. Maybe not. However, in my opinion, it doesn't mean you're not in love anymore. It means you're not willing to risk your relationship by having an affair. If you are willing to go through with this, it means you are taking on a challenge so you can stay close to your partner. That's what swinging is really all about. Keeping and staying close with the one you love, yet allowing them (and yourself) the freedom to explore their sexuality.

How do you define love? Is it a feeling of warmth or is it white-hot sweaty sex, two souls intermingling? Love can be acceptance; it can be trust. It can be a good feeling whenever you're around the one you love. *The definition of love depends on your definition of love.*

Love is the foundation to any good relationship, whether it's an open one or not. Without love for your partner, swinging really doesn't work. If you feel indifference for your partner and go into swinging, it might change your feelings. I have known people who have fallen in love all over again because they started swinging. I have also known people who have broken up because of it. There has to be some measure of love there for it to work.

Keep in mind it's all a matter of perspective. And don't doubt yourself so much.

Broaching the subject.

This is one of the hardest things to do. To tell your partner you're interested in swinging is worse than going to the dentist for a root canal. A lot worse. Just talking about this subject can be a very difficult thing to do. It is a nerve wracking, heart pumping, nail biting thing. It means putting yourself on the chopping block and maybe jeopardizing your relationship. It's just hard to admit to the person whom you love that you want to fuck other people or that you want to watch *them* fuck other people. There really is no easy way to do it. It's going to be hard.

As they say, no pain, no gain.

If you've decided to do it, it is recommended that you approach your lover with love and understanding. Don't start out by making accusations about their feelings, such as how you know they would like to have sex with other people. For all you know, they don't.

Keep in mind that they might not go for the idea and they might freak out. They might be hurt. This is a risk you have to take. You know your partner best. You should have a feeling about whether or not they're going to go for the idea. And if they do, great. Swinging is a fantastic experience couples can share. And if they don't go for the idea, don't be disheartened. Remember, you are in an important relationship with someone you care a great deal about. This is more important than swinging. And, you never know, they could change their mind at a later date.

You're probably afraid to bring the subject up. You might be apprehensive because you think your partner will think you're a pervert or that you don't love them anymore. My advice? Ease into it. It won't be easy. You *have* to be willing to put yourself on the line and bring it to the table.

You know your partner best. And you know if you can bring it up. The most important message of this book is that the swinging Lifestyle is not for everyone. You should know going in that they might not go for the idea. Even if it makes perfect sense to you to do it, it might make perfect sense to them *not* to do it.

Are you an open-minded person? What about your partner? Look for signs. Women usually do the subtle hinting such as talking about other men being good looking. With men, it's different. Most men want sex with other women, so bringing up this subject to them shouldn't be all that difficult. Most men, unless extremely jealous and insecure, will jump at the idea. It's a fact of life. It's the way they're built, so get over it. We wouldn't want them any other way.

Remember, if you don't ever ask, you'll never know. No guts no glory. And, you're not getting any younger.

On the flip side, your partner may be waiting for you to bring to subject up first. You never know.

More often than not, talking is the best method. Bring it up casually, maybe as a joke, "Look at us, we're like a bunch of swingers or something." Start dropping the term swinging into your conversations. Ask them casually, "Have you ever heard of swinging?" Or, "What do you think about people who swing?" Be aware that they might not know what you're talking about. It may seem unfathomable, but many people out there haven't heard of swinging. They don't have a clue as to what it really is about.

Watch their reactions. Do not expect them to be overjoyed at first. Many people are apprehensive. It's natural. Pay attention to their responses. They may find it threatening. They may be angry that you'd bring up "such an idea". Be prepared for this.

Take it slow. Approach it delicately. But know there is no easy way to do it. No matter how much you prepare, they may feel as though you're blurting it out. It may sound right in your head, "*I want to fuck other people,*" but once someone else hears it, it may seem like a slight shock.

Some suggestions:
- Talk about people you find attractive.
- Talk about unrealized fantasies.
- Ask them about *their* unrealized fantasies.
- Read adult magazines advice columns aloud to them and ask, "What do you think of that?"
- Tell then a naughty story you heard or made up. (Let your imagination run wild.)

Look for signs. How are they responding? Get it done and move forward. Don't waste a lot of time preparing to do it. You don't know until you ask. And you have to ask.

If they are warming up to the idea (and you'll know if they are) go for it. You could ask something like, "Have you ever thought about having sex with other people?" If they are human, they have. They might turn the question right back on you, "Have *you*?" This is your ticket. Be honest. "Well, yeah, sometimes."

This would the time to tell them there is a way to have sex with other people without jeopardizing your relationship. Tell them what you know about it. Keep yourself in check and don't act too excited or too nervous. Let the conversation go where it may. If it ends in a fight, and be warned that it might, take time to cool off. I might even suggest waiting for them to bring it back up to you. If they never do, it's not a good sign that they're loving the idea.

And let the chips fall where they may. *Give them time to absorb the information.*

It may take months or even years for them to warm up to the idea. It may not. Swinging is about mutual sexual exploration. However one partner may be more sexually adventurous than the other. This is not unusual. Hold their hand and tell them you'll be there for them.

However, if they are responding favorably, go for it. Do some research. Go into it together, as a unit. Never leave any information, no matter how minute, out. Never hid it. Swinging is about being honest with each other.

Related experience:

This is Jeff's story:

"I had wanted to try swinging for years, mainly because the thought of my wife getting fucked by another man was extremely erotic to me. But I didn't have the balls to bring it up.

One night, we were in bed spooning and we were about to have sex. I don't know why, but I began to trace lines along her body and I began to whisper in her ear, telling her how sexy she was. I kept whispering and we were getting really aroused. But she didn't move. She just laid there and enjoyed the sensations from my hands. I found myself thinking about her fucking another guy and it was too much. Before I could stop myself, I whispered, 'I'd love to see you get fucked by another man.' She moaned in response and I knew, just knew she liked the idea too."

That's one way to bring it up. A very good way, in fact. Here's another.

Related experience:

A friend of mine told me how she broached the subject with her husband. (I like to call it *The Blunt Approach.*) They had only been married a few years, but both were into their thirties and, as she put it, "Time was running out! I had to do this."

So, she got him drunk one night and started talking about other women.

"Honey, do you think she's pretty?" she asked about an actress on the television.

Of course, being the smart man he is, he replied, "She's okay, but not as pretty as you."

She then told him, "Brad Pitt. I think he's hot. I'd do him in a minute."

Her husband eyed her and said, "Really?"

"Yeah," she said. "I really would, but he's not the only guy I'd like to do. I mean, you know, if I wasn't married."

He nodded for her to continue.

"I'd like to do Steve."

Steve is her husband's best friend.

"Steve?!" he half-yelled. "You're kidding?"

"No, I'm not. And I know you'd like to do Mindy."

She works with Mindy.

"No I wouldn't!"

She eyed him and nodded. "Yes, you would. I know and it's cool. I'd like to do Mindy myself.

"Oh, really?" he asked.

"Yeah," she said. "I dunno, it just makes me tingle to think of other girls. I'm just curious to know what that's all about."

His eyes nearly popped out of his head.

"So," she said. "What do you think?"

"I'm kinda curious about you and another girl, too."

He has such a great sense of humor. They started swinging shortly thereafter.

I think we can take a cue from her. She broached the subject by making an off-handed statement, "*I'd do Brad Pitt.*" Well, quite honestly, most women *would*. Yet, she took it a step farther and asked him who *he'd* do.

Remember: Lack of pressure and loving support.

The most important thing is don't be pushy! Don't try to bully them into giving it a try. Mutual consent or nothing. You can't talk someone into it. They have to go for the idea. If they don't, they don't. Nothing you can do about it.

What happens if they say no to swinging? They say no. What did you lose? You never know until you try, so just be glad that they've been honest with you. It's important to know that if you're not suited for this lifestyle and you go into it blindly without knowing the true feelings of yourself and your partner, you can experience a lot of pain because of it. Swinging is highly emotionally charged.

If you still want to give it a try and they don't, all I can tell you is that it's probably not going to work. It could happen but more than likely it won't. Just let them know how much *you* love *them*. Tell them your relationship means more than swinging. Assure them. These things take time. Be willing to put that time in. But don't waste a lot of mental effort in trying to "convince" them to do it. You can't convince someone, they have to make that decision for themselves.

What happens if they say yes? Congratulations! You're half-way there, baby! Get ready, though. It may be a bumpy ride, but be assured, one well worth it.

And after you're done with "The Talk" you might even have some really great sex afterwards. Enjoy it. You deserve it. Swinging can bring the animal out in you. And in your partner. You've been warned.

A few questions to ask yourself.

- Why do I want this?
- What benefit do I hope to get out of it?
- Am I able to handle changes in my relationship?
- What are my expectations?
- What are my partner's expectations?
- How is my current sex life?
- Am I doing this for the right reasons, i.e. because I want to do it or because it's something my partner wants me to do?
- Do I think it will save my relationship?
- Do I think it will ruin my relationship?
- Do I think it's wrong?

Swinging is not a question of right and wrong. It's a question of if it's right or wrong *for you*.

Is swinging a lifestyle choice?

"Lifestyle" is such a heavy word. As if everything as you know it *has* to change once you make the decision to swing. But *is* it a lifestyle choice?

Not necessarily. For some reason, people get it into their heads that swinging is a complete lifestyle change. It's really not. Most swingers do it whenever they want and still maintain every aspect of their "normal" lives. Swinging is usually just an addition to their everyday routines. It's out of the ordinary but not abnormal. It's something they enjoy but they don't allow it to take precedence over their lives.

It *can* be a lifestyle choice in the sense that it can change your life as you know it *if you want it to*. But it doesn't have to be a complete overhaul of your existing life.

It might simply be a hobby, something you do occasionally for fun. You might get into it and it becomes a regular part of your routine, something you participate in every weekend. You might get into it and go months between swinging, maybe even years. People take breaks all the time. You might only want to go to the occasional party or have the occasional date. You might do it once and never want to do it again. You might not ever actually have sex with other people but go to parties regularly.

And, of course, some swingers do make it their life. They may plan their vacations around it. They may start clubs or throw regular parties. Some run dating websites, start swing travel agencies. They, in essence, provided the infrastructure for the rest of us to swing. While it's not necessary for everyone to become this involved, without these people, swinging would be a lot more difficult.

Remember: *Your level of participation is entirely up to you.*

When and if you decide to do it, make it count. If you go into it expecting nothing to happen, more than likely it won't. You must put yourself out there. People will not come to you because they don't know you or your level of participation and experience.

Be sure not to over analyze situations. Just do what *feels* right.

Agreements.

As long as you and your partner agree, swinging can be free of rules. That's the great thing about it. There are no set rules. It's different for everyone. You can do whatever with whomever and still come home to the greatest girl/boy on earth. Well, there's a little more to it than that...

It should be noted that, in the midst of all this pleasure, there should be a few ground rules. It is my personal opinion that if you have more than five rules, you are not ready to swing.

But before you begin, you need to set a few rules down *on paper.* You can call this your *Swinging Agreement* between you and your partner.

These are a few basic rules most people have:
- Please tell me if you are leaving the room with someone.
- Please use condoms.

Your rules will vary, of course and that's okay. The point is for you to know what you can and can't do.

Personal experience:
We'd been swinging for about a year, with many rules and agreements. As we were on our way to a party, and with a burst of inspiration, I came up with the idea of throwing all the rules out the window. My husband agreed. We agreed that anything that went down that night, we'd deal with in the morning whatever the consequences. To our utter delight, it turned out to be the best party we'd ever been to.

I found myself dancing in the nude with other women and he found himself getting busy in one of the bedrooms. We ended up in a threesome with another girl. It was awesome, to say the least.

At the end of the night, we went back to our hotel room, arm in arm and had some fantastic sex. I don't think I've ever been more turned on in my life than I was that night.

We threw out the rulebook. And that's what can happen when you throw out the rulebook.

So, sometimes, it's just easier to not have rules.

Your own rules may be different according to your circumstances. You may only be into the soft swing (doing everything except actual intercourse).You may only be allowed to hook up if your partner does. Whatever rules you have, make sure *both parties understand and agree to them.*

Of course, there will be times that your partner does things you never thought they would. They may break your agreement or go against your rules. Be prepared. It may shock you at first. On the other hand, *you* might do something they never thought you would do. Normally, for a strong couple, this only enhances the experience. For some, it seems like a betrayal.

Related experience:
This is Kelly's story.

"It was the second time we'd swung with this couple. We did a full swap. Things went well that night and when they offered to let us stay the night at their house, we readily agreed. I got in bed and my husband went to get a drink of water. I drifted off but was awakened a minute later by sounds of lovemaking. My husband was not in the room with me. I was like, *What the hell...?* I soon realized the three of them were having a threesome, without inviting me. I was, to say the least, mortified and, no this wasn't in our rules. In fact, I had never even considered anything like this happening.

I laid there and I just didn't know what to do. Should I go in there and ask them to stop? We were both into the same room sex thing so this wasn't in our rules. I couldn't believe my husband would do that and that *they* would overstep their boundaries like that.

Well, it just seemed as though it went on forever but I couldn't find the courage to stop it because I didn't want to seem like a wet blanket. But it did hurt me, him doing that. I never expected that out of him and when he finally came into the room, I was so hurt, I was crying. He asked what was wrong and I told him he shouldn't have done that and he said, 'Well, we never said we couldn't do it. You can do it if you like.'

I told him we were leaving and we told the other couple we had an early appointment we'd forgotten about. Once we were in the car, I laid into him. And you know what he said? He said, 'You could have joined us if you wanted to!' Whatever. We stopped swinging after that. Maybe I just couldn't handle it. Or maybe they were just being selfish assholes."

Kelly had a limit she didn't even know she had. She had never thought about something like that happening. And once it happened, she couldn't handle it.

This happens a lot. People go into swinging with certain expectations and when they're not met, they quit. It's cool. I'll say it again, swinging isn't for everyone. We all have our boundaries. That is why it is so important to plan *before* you do something. Feelings can get so easily hurt when you're doing something like this and no matter how fun it can be— and it can be really fun—there are times when things are out of your control.

Fun for all.

First of all, if you've been together for a while, you might have stopped having fun as a couple.

I know there is always some other something going on that is always keeping you from doing stuff together. That's life. However, if you are going to swing, you might need to reacquaint yourselves with one another. And that means re-learning to have fun together.

Swinging is all about couple fun. If you can't have fun together before you start swinging, it's unlikely you will afterwards.

Let's start with the three basics: Porn, masturbation and, of course, sex toys.

Porn.

One of the best ways to get reacquainted is to watch porn together. It amazes me at the number of couples that do not watch adult videos. Why? It may surprise you to know that pornography is as strong an aphrodisiac as any other. (Oysters do not compare.) Watching porn can really get you going. I've had a ton of great sex before, during and after watching porn. If you don't want to go to a video store, there are a ton of sites on the internet that sell videos and you can have them delivered to your door anonymously.

Masturbation.

Let's repeat this together. Masturbation is good for you. Masturbation is good for you.

So, whether or not you're doing it is a good indicator of whether or not you're going to be able to swing. While some people, especially men, start masturbating at puberty, some do not start masturbating until their late teens or even twenties, and some never do. I once met a couple who insisted neither of them *ever* masturbated. Flabbergasted, I had to ask, "*Why not?*" They couldn't really answer. They said they were swingers, too. (I'm still trying to figure that one out.)

Another good thing indicator is whether or not your lover masturbates. How does that make you feel? Personally, I feel kind of indifferent, but if he told he didn't *do* it, I'd get worried. There's just something about people who don't masturbate that worries me.

The message is, if you are not in touch with your own sexuality and how to stimulate yourself to orgasm, how on earth can you be in touch with someone else's? Masturbation is about self love, first and foremost. And once you learn to love yourself in that way, you can share it with others.

Sex toys.

I just wanted to mention this briefly because there are still a lot of people out there who do not have any sex toys. One great way for a couple to learn to play together is with sex toys. Incorporate them into your regular sex. Toys are a lot of fun, so just let your imagination run wild. Women, let him have the control a few times and get wild. Just lay there and let him do *whatever* he wants to do with your body. It is so nice. Or, make him watch you pleasure yourself. Men really get off by watching their lover masturbate herself to orgasm.

Also, for those of you who love doggie sex, but can't seem to come doing it, place a vibrator on your clitoris as you're doing it (or have him hold it for you.) The double stimulation is out of this world!

Of course, going solo with a sex toy can be just as good. Take time to explore your sexuality. Sex toys are a great way to get started.

Some other really good stuff to do together:
- Get naked around each other. (Be sure to draw the curtains.)
- Take naked pictures of each other. (Put them in a safe place!)
- Find a secluded area at a lake or a beach and go skinny dipping. If you get caught, laugh it off. It *is* funny! (TRY NOT TO GET CAUGHT!)
- Go on the internet and look up some adult sites. (Many sites have free picture galleries.) Talk about who you find attractive and would love to have sex with.
- Use pet names for each other. "Sexy" is always good.
- Go into an adult bookstore together and buy some fun stuff.
- Turn on the stereo and dance together. (Dancing is a big part of swinging.)
- Tell each other your sexual fantasies.
- Tell each other stuff you'd like to do with other people. (It could just be the touching. A lot of people go into swinging because they simply like to touch other people.)
- If possible, go to a nudist colony or resort. You'll see that it's not that big of a deal. You'll wonder what you were scared of.
- Talk about why you want to swing. Be honest.
- Read erotica and then discuss.

- Go to a bar and then separate. Spend an hour or so flirting with other people. Meet up and discuss your findings.
- Always tell each other when you've been checked out by another person. ("That chick just checked out my ass!" Or "Honey, a guy whistled at me today!")
- Take a long drive together at night.
- Tell each other what you like about one another.
- Go to a drive-in.
- Give full body massages.
- Sleep in the nude.
- Go to church together and pray for your souls. (Obviously this one is a joke. *Lighten up!* If you're going to swing, you are gong to have to develop a sense of humor.)
- Tell each other jokes and laugh your asses off.

Strip clubs: Men's entertainment or marital aid?

One way to gauge if you're ready for the Lifestyle or not might be to take your partner to a strip club. Chances are, if they can't handle going to one, then there is no way they are going to be able to handle swinging.

There is an entrance fee to get in a club and the drinks can be expensive. If you want a private dance or show, that can be expensive as well. It might be a good idea to just leave your credit cards at home and just take cash. That way, you won't be too tempted to overspend. (I say this because I have a male friend that finds himself in credit card debt any time he goes to a strip club. The next day, he kicks himself in the ass.)

The thing to know is that you don't have to drink that much nor do you have to buy a lapdance once you get there. Many people just go in and watch the strippers onstage. And most go up to the stage and tip. Be sure to bring a lot of one dollar bills with you.

Personal experience:
The first time I went into a strip club, I had my husband and a close, male friend with me. I was so nervous. I didn't have a clue as to what to expect. After we entered and sat down, I was immediately fascinated with all the strippers. They all walked around semi-nude so comfortably. They had confidence. And they were very interested in me. When I

went to tip for the first time, the stripper gave me a little extra dance and the men in there loved it. The DJ even said, "Don't you love it when the girls play together?" It was one of the best times I've ever had and when we got home, we had some really hot sex.

So, screw up your courage and enjoy a night at a club. Remember, the strippers are there making a living and have no interest in anyone's husband or boyfriend.

More questions.

Answer these questions and *be completely honest.*

- How is your current sex life?
- Are you satisfied with your sex life?
- Why do you want to swing? Variety? The feeling of missing out on something?
- Have you ever experienced a mind-blowing orgasm?
- After sex are you hot, sweaty and panting or just glad it's over? Are you content? Do you want to do it again ASAP?
- Do you love your partner?
- Have you ever experimented with sex toys, lubes, anal sex, etc.?
- Have you ever slept in the nude?
- Do you take showers together with your partner?
- When was the last time you and your partner did something together without anyone else? Was it fun?
- When was the last time you gave or received a massage from your partner?
- Can you openly discuss sex with your partner?
- Have you ever posed for "dirty" pictures?
- Have you ever video taped yourself having sex?

If you've got more no's than yes's, then you might want to consider turning those no's into yes's before you proceed.

Being nude. Can you handle it?

When you go to any swing party or club, there is going to be lots of nudity. Sometimes I wonder if most people swing just so they can get naked. (It's a perk for me anyway.) All of us are exhibitionists to a certain extent and being allowed to get naked and free is a definite plus to swinging.

Personally, it took me a while to warm up to being nude around other people. I took it slow at first (just taking off my top, then bra, then my pants...you get the picture) and now I love being naked. For me, it's so liberating. And after that initial shock of *"I'm naked!"* it just seems downright silly to be hung up on it.

One way to prepare yourself is to walk around your house in the nude. If you have kids, why not get a hotel room and sit around all night naked? Another good way is to sleep in the nude but be warned, once you start this, you won't be able to go back to pajamas.

Sitting on the fence. Should you or shouldn't you?

If you're still reading, you are more than interested in swinging, but you may still be sitting on the fence. So should you or shouldn't you? *Again, the decision to do it is entirely your own.*

If you're still interested, it's now time for you to take actual measures and get the ball rolling.

Is swinging morally wrong?

Everyone has morality issues with something. Swingers experience it, too. In fact it was the one the toughest issues for me when I began to consider it, having been raised in a strict religious background. You might be asking yourself the same question. *Is it wrong?*

In my opinion, it's not wrong. What's wrong with it? Ask yourself that. If you come up with a million reasons not to do it, then don't do it. It's not for you. But if you can't think of a real reason other than the banal "it's wrong", this might be a good choice for you and your partner.

One way you might want to consider looking at it is like this. Say someone divorces five or six times. *Five or six times.* They're not marrying the love of their lives each time. Most likely, they're switching sex partners under the premise of "doing it the right way" by marrying. Think of all the time and money and emotional baggage they have to go through in order just to sleep with someone else. It's not only unnecessary when you get right down to it, it's also pretty stupid.

I believe if more people would give swinging a chance, the divorce rate would go down. A little radical? Maybe. But consider this: People divorce for a number of reasons, but what they won't say is, *I really want to fuck other people.* You can't say that out loud, you can't tell anyone that, but, more than likely, it's the real reason.

On the other hand, it's okay for a single person to go around and fuck everything that moves. Right? But a person who is either married or has a long-term committed relationship isn't allowed this luxury. You made the decision to get into that relationship, so you're stuck with it and the burden of not being able to have some extra sex. Most times, people in long-term relationships need it more than single people.

If you're single, you're allowed to be sexually promiscuous. If you're committed to a relationship, you have to pretty much let that part of your sexuality die. And the problem is, for most of us, it never dies. The smart ones try swinging or an open relationship. The other less adventurous ones cheat on their lovers. They can't face up to their true desires. They can't be honest with their partners. Cheating is an alternative, though most times it ends in disaster. And once is never enough. Once a cheater, always a cheater. And why is cheating so tantalizing? *Because it feels good* to have sex with other people. That's why people normally do it.

If I've heard it once, I've heard it a thousand times, "I don't know what came over me! It just happened!" More than likely, it *did* just happen. Sex is natural and when you're presented with the opportunity to do it, you will want to do it. It's almost unnatural *not* to do it.

So which is better? Being honest about your desires or being dishonest and hurting other people?

Whatever the reason you want to swing, let it be your own.

The green-eyed monster.

Unfortunately, jealousy is a big part of swinging.

In an ideal world, there would be no jealousy. We could all love one another without restriction, without regret and without jealousy. However, we all know we do not live in an ideal world and, to be honest, who would really want to? How boring would that be? Sure, you are going to experience jealousy. If you don't, you're not human. Expect it. A little jealousy shouldn't stop you from doing what you want to do nor should you let it control you.

The important thing to remember is what you will gain if you overcome your jealousy. Know that confronting your insecurities will be worth it. It will help you to be a better person.

So, expect a little jealousy from yourself, from your partner and from other people. The key is how you handle it.

Personal experience:
We knew this couple and saw them on and off for about a year. We usually did full swap/same room sex with them. We always had a good time. Until...

One night he and I finished first and were about to leave the room to go smoke a cigarette when she moaned my partner's name.

It made me so jealous I couldn't see straight. *She just moaned my lover's name!* I thought I was the only one who got to do that! It was just *too* personal for me.

I refused to see them ever again. It may sound silly, but that's the one thing I don't want to hear. Yes, enjoy him and have fun, but don't get too personal. She had crossed my boundary.

She probably didn't even know she did it. It just came out. Things like this happen all the time. I never even considered that something this minute would get to me. But it did.

You have to be a pretty strong individual to swing. We all have our pet peeves and swinging can bring out the worse in everyone if you're not careful to keep yourself in check.

I try not to pay so much attention if I finish first.

On the other hand, this should be mentioned. Many men go into swinging thinking that they are going to get to screw whomever they want, whenever they want. They say, "Let's try swinging," thinking that this will help them get more sex.

What many of these men don't count on is that they're not in control of swinging. *Women are.* Many men are not able to handle it. They see their women out there getting hit on left and right and sometimes, they feel left out. They see their lovers having fun and if they focus too much on it, the green-eyed monster will eat them alive.

It's not only that they are jealous of their lover, they are jealous that their lover is having more fun and more opportunity to have sex than they are. They feel left out of the loop.

Women call the shots. Men are not in control, especially at swing parties and clubs. Men don't approach women. They have to wait for the woman to give the sign. If men approach women, they have to do it very delicately. Most times, many men just wait for a woman to approach them. And if they don't, they don't. That's just the way it works.

While, on the surface, this may seem a little weird, it's true.

Related experience:

"It was the first time my wife and I had been to a club. We got there and all of a sudden, she was getting hit on by every man and woman in there.

I was shocked. I was also pretty pissed off. No one paid any attention to me. It was all about her. And she flirted with everyone. She was suddenly transformed before my very eyes. She was a new person who was desirable to the entire world. And I was just the bum who was with her.

I just kept thinking, *She's such a slut! She's such a slut!* And it didn't set well with me. Even though I was the one who wanted to swing in the first place, and I had basically talked her into it, I just felt left out and undesirable. And she was like girl of the hour or something. Everyone wanted to be with her. I couldn't handle it. I wanted to have as much (if not more) fun than she was having. I know I've got a hot wife but I never actually thought everyone would want to fuck her. It was too much to handle.

I was such an idiot. I sat down and pouted. She ignored me, as she should have. When she went into a room with another couple, I couldn't handle it. I jumped up and went in there and told her I was ready to leave. When we got into the car, I tore into her. And she started crying, 'You wanted this! Not me!' And she was right. I was such a dick to her.

I finally calmed down and apologized to her. She was just so new to me. I never realized this was the way it would be. I thought we'd both have lots of fun. I didn't realize how in control women are in swing situations. Being a man, I'm used to pulling the strings, but in swinging if you try it, you just end up looking like a prick. Like I did.

I finally got sorted out and we tried it again. We went to a club and she stayed by my side all night. She held my hand through it. She told me she loved me and it didn't matter if she did anything or not. This made me feel worse. I told her to go and have fun. I just ignored her the entire night. I had to do that to get through it. I made out with a cute girl but I kept thinking about what *she* was doing. It sounds stupid, but I felt like I was giving her away to the world. But I was sure as hell relieved when she came back to me.

That was years ago, when I really didn't understand what swinging was all about and how it worked. Once I got it figured out, I realized what a lucky man I am to have such a desirable wife. But it did scare me at first because I was almost afraid she'd figure out she didn't need me and that she could have all this fun on her own. That's just paranoia, though. And, as with the jealousy, I got through it. Thank God."

Again, be prepared. You don't know until you try it, but knowing what to expect can make a difference.

Hooking up via the World Wide Web.

The quickest and easiest way to find out about clubs and dating is on the internet. There are plenty of sites that offer good information. All you have to do is find a search engine and type in "*swinging*", "*open relationships*" or "*couple swapping*".

I pretty much figure that if you're reading this book, you've already done this but I wanted to be sure to include this bit of information for those of you who haven't.

After you've made the decision to swing, you might want to place an online ad in search of other couples. Lots of people, including myself, use this tool to meet and contact other like-minded people.

Placing an online ad isn't very complicated. It's almost like placing a classified in a newspaper. I would suggest you sit down and talk about it with your partner first. Decide what you want to say about yourselves. Read other ads and get a feel for it. Type it up on your word processing program first and let it sit a day, then go back and revise, if necessary.

Then put it up and see what kind of responses you get. It's very exciting when you first do it. I think I checked my mailbox a zillion times a day after we placed our first ad.

Do you want to include a picture with your ad? It's a personal choice, but do what makes *you* comfortable. Many people do not have a picture included in their ads. And if they do, their faces are usually blacked out. It's okay to do this as long as the picture shows your body. It gives people an idea of what you look like. You can send a real picture later after you start corresponding with a couple you're interested in.

On the other hand, if you do want to include a picture on your ad, don't insult everyone by taking a picture of your genitals and posting them. That's not a very pleasant way to say "hello", is it? For some reason, many couples post these kinds of pictures. I don't know why. Sure, sex is a big part of it and it does include genitalia, yet these kinds of pictures are just so impersonal. I have heard numerous complaints about this. Faces and bodies are what do it, not genitals. Faces and bodies get people interested in you. People will want to know what *you* look like. If they are not attracted to your face and body, more than likely they won't be attracted to your penis or vagina. Also, some people consider it rude to be sent via email a picture of a couple having sex which only shows the penis and vagina.

When you are contacted by a couple, or you contact a couple, it is customary to include a picture of yourself and your partner. *Be sure to include both parties.* Both of you will be swinging, after all. There are many times couples just send a picture of the female, which is great, but if the male plans on joining in, he needs to show his face as well.

The pictures I like best are where the couples are just facing the camera and smiling. They are dressed in tasteful clothing. (You can get a good reading on people by seeing how they're dressed.) If you don't have any sexy clothes, buy some. You might even want to consider purchasing a digital camera because you'll want to update your pictures from time to time.

After you've got your clothing situation under control, play dress up. Do your make-up as if you were going out for a night on the town. Men should always shave. Set the camera up in a nicely decorated place with *plenty of light.* Be sure to take a picture standing up and sitting down. And say cheese!

Sending a picture online might make you uncomfortable. If this is the case, you might not be ready to swing. This is a big part of it. People will want to know what you look like. And one of the most annoying things in the world is to be contacted by a couple who refuse to send a picture. What's the big deal? If we met, wouldn't I find out what they look like? I know we tend to be overly cautious in this crazy world of ours, but if you're going to swing, you're going to have to get over some of these hang-ups.

How about contacting someone whose ad you've ran across? What do you say? Be simple and straightforward. Don't be afraid. *They know why you've contacted them.* Tell your ages, your interests and maybe what brought you to swinging (realizing fantasies, etc.) and where you're located. (You do not have to give specific addresses. Just tell them the vicinity.) Three or four lines should do it. No one wants to hear your life story in an initial email.

My best advice is to send a picture with your initial contact email. This way, they see you and if they like what they see, they'll respond. And if not, you won't have to spend days swapping emails and waiting for them to make up their minds. If you don't hear from them in a few days, move on to another couple. If they don't answer back quickly, they won't be worth dealing with. Trust me on this one.

Don't get hung up on one couple. Don't think you have to have a perfect match. Don't let your feelings get hurt if they don't respond. Move on.

Fakers.

One warning: If someone wants "dirty" pictures, think twice before sending them. While this is "done", there are a lot of people out there who just want to swap pictures for the purpose of seeing naked people. This person could a minor or just a dirty old man. Realize that the possibility exists that it's not a real swinger couple. Use your gut instinct.

One of the main problems with meeting other couples online is that there are a large number of fakers out there. The majority of the fakers are single men posing as couples. They do this because they want your naked pictures. They might even send you a few of themselves, which, of course, is not really them, but usually a picture they stole off of an internet site somewhere or tricked some other couple into sending them.

How to tell if you have a faker on your hands:
- They don't answer any personal questions.
- They are overly interested.
- They want you to send more than one picture.
- When you ask to meet them, they always have other plans.
- The picture they sent you just doesn't look right. It might look like a model. It probably is.

Personal experience:
We were swapping pics with what we assumed was an interested swinging couple. The male always wanted to

cyber, too. Which was cool, at first, but after a while, you just don't have that much time. One day, my partner was on the internet and saw that the couple was online. He instant-messaged them to be nice because the husband was always instant messaging us. This time it was his wife.

She sent a message back that confused my husband: "Who are you?"

He was perplexed but told her he was part of the couple she'd been swapping pics with and emailing. She didn't know anything about this. Her husband had been emailing us her nude pics without her knowledge. And getting mine! UGH!

A faker will eventually lose interest in you and move on to victimize another couple. More than likely, they're harmless, but they are annoying. No one likes to be made a fool of.

On the other side of this, you also have couples who are not interested in swinging but get their kicks cybering, exchanging dirty emails and pictures. That's okay if they're upfront and honest about it. They usually are not and have no intention of ever meeting you, only wasting your time. Spotting this particular breed is difficult. But if you've been emailing for over two weeks with no real talk of meeting, you're probably wasting your time.

Related experience:

This is a friend's story.

"We were emailing back and forth with this couple who said we were everything they were looking for and couldn't wait to meet us. They also wanted to tell us all their fantasies, in explicit detail and they wanted us to tell them about our fantasies as well. Sure, why not? My fantasy has always been a threesome, with another woman and my husband. We'd cyber for hours about this particular fantasy and they agreed we could give it a try when we met. I couldn't wait to meet them because I was dying to do it. I could just taste it I wanted it so bad. I had been with a few women at that point and wanted to share that with my partner. I could just see us three in front of a fireplace on a bearskin rug.

I kept trying to set a date, and they kept sidestepping me. After a while it just got old. I asked them to please set a date and never heard from them again. Go figure. We'd been had. They got their kicks through dirty emails and cybering. That's okay, but it's not how I get *my* kicks. I'm a swinger and I like to get laid. In reality."

Keep in mind that this happens to the best of us. Don't take it personally. Move on.

Swinging costs money.

I have had a blast swinging but sometimes I find myself counting the dollars we have spent to enjoy the Lifestyle. Whether you are going on a date, attending a party or going to a club, expect to spend money.

You will usually have to travel to meet other swingers and bear in mind that the world is a big place. In America alone, depending on where you live, it's not uncommon to find yourself traveling upwards of two-hundred miles or more to meet a couple. You just have to ask yourself if you can afford it and if it's going to be worth it.

It usually is.

Costs that can be incurred:
- Hotels.
- Gasoline.
- Plane tickets (if necessary to travel to a convention, party, etc...)
- Meals. (Most swingers meet in nice restaurants. You don't want to meet someone at McDonald's, do you?)
- Cost of entrance to a party or club.
- Cost of condoms and birth control. (Don't scrimp on this!)
- New clothing.
- Manicures, pedicures, beauty treatments so you can look good.
- Parking.

- Drinks.
- Babysitters.

Of course, if you have a successful swing experience, it will be well worth it. But be prepared to spend some money before you actually find a good match.

This is what we do. We put a few dollars back per week for this purpose. A *Swing Fund*, if you will. It doesn't have to be much, say twenty dollars or so. That way, when an event comes up that we would like to attend it doesn't cut into our normal expenses.

Of course, you might be financially secure and don't have to worry about this aspect. Congratulations on that. But I know a lot of people who've had to turn down invites because they didn't have the money. It's a fact of life and needs to be pointed out.

Another thing to keep in mind is that sometimes another couple might offer to pick up the tab. I don't recommend this. It just really gets things off to a weird start. Pay for everything yourself and if you become friends, then you (or they) can pick up the tab at a later date. People can get weird about money and swinging isn't about money. It's about sex.

Dating.

Yes, this is essentially what you are going to be doing. Swinging is like dating. Don't expect to click with everyone you meet. And don't expect to like all of them. On the other hand, don't expect everyone to like you, either. That's expecting too much.

Alternatively, don't be too picky. You're not going to marry these people and most people are not perfect. Expectation always outweighs reality. Remember that.

One good way to ease yourself into it is to check out a swinger's message board on the internet. You can find tons of good message boards where you can discuss your feelings, fears and anxieties. Most couples experience the same feelings about swinging and it's good to share that with others. It's good to know there are other people out there who are going through the same thing you are.

There are plenty of people on these boards who have been swinging for a while and they are usually more than willing to dispense advice. Give them a try. You might even meet a great couple off of a message board. (Be warned, many message boards do not allow personal ads, so please don't place an ad on one of these. Always use the ad section.)

After you've found a couple and decide to meet, you are going to be nervous. Expect that.

A few things to think about:

- Expect to be nervous.
- *Don't drink too much. This is a biggie and one that can easily happen due to nervousness.*
- Be yourself.
- If you don't click with this couple try again with a different couple. It's really no biggie.

Give yourself permission to go slow at first. Do not jump right into anything your first time unless it feels right. Give yourself time to ease into it. *Don't rush.*

Remember, if the Lifestyle is right for you, you will have many more opportunities to swing. The first date should be enjoyed for the new experience it is. And, your first date is nerve racking enough without adding sex to the equation. It is important to know that you don't have to jump right in and have sex with the first couple you meet. You should be relatively comfortable with them before this happens. However, if you find yourself feeling very comfortable on the first date, you might want to go for it. It's all up to the individuals involved.

However, if you go on a date and decide this is *not* the couple you want to swing with, make your excuses and leave after dinner or drinks. A simple, "I have to get up early tomorrow for work" or something to that effect usually works. You don't have to go into a lengthy explanation of why you don't want to swing with them. It's unnecessary and sometimes quite rude. Be polite because you might change your mind at a later date and decide that you want to swing with them.

Where should you meet for the first time? It depends on what you and the other couple wants to do. You could meet for drinks at a bar. Or you could have dinner in a nice restaurant. You could meet up and go to a club together. It's your decision. But my advice is to meet somewhere you can talk privately without a lot of distractions. (And noise.)

We always like to meet new people in early afternoon before restaurants and bars get too busy. That way, if we want to do anything, none of us will be too tired to actually do it.

After the introductions, what should you talk about? Pop culture is a good ice breaker. Talk about the menu items or what kinds of drinks they like.

Remember these are people like you meet everyday. Talk to them like you do everybody else. Don't try to commandeer the conversation and give everyone a chance to speak.

So, screw up your courage, relax and don't put a lot of pressure on yourself. Enjoy it for what it is: A precursor to many more new and exciting experiences.

Making the first move.

The first thing to remember is that you are, in fact, on a date with another couple. They are interviewing you as you, in turn, are interviewing them. Be open, friendly and nice. They know why you're there: You possibly want to have sex with them. If the topic of swinging comes up (it should at some point), don't try to steer it away from the conversation. This is what you're there for. Most times, this takes the edge off and everyone gets a good laugh. If it makes you *that* nervous, you might not be ready to swing.

The key thing to remember is that they are as nervous as you are. Don't try to hide it; it's a human thing.

Personal experience:
The first couple we met were the nicest people around, though we ended up not swinging with them.

We were all extremely nervous on our first date and then on the second, we didn't have time to actually have sex. So, by the third date, we knew each other too well and it would have just not seemed right. The guy began to remind me of one of my old boyfriends and I just couldn't see us together in that way after so many dates. They also lived a long way away and we had to travel a great distance to meet them. We still email each other a lot even though nothing ever happened.

Persistence pays off in the long run, but if you wait too long, you might begin to see the other couple only as *friends*.

This doesn't happen to everyone, but it is a possibility. And we all know it's hard to fuck your friends.

I would say by the second or third date, if not by the first, you should know whether or not you'll want to have sex with them.

It's good to take time to get to know another couple, but just don't miss that window of opportunity or you might not have another chance to jump through it again. The other couple could change their minds and stop swinging or *you* could change your mind. You never know. Don't let opportunity slip away because of anxiety. Live through the feelings as they will pass. And get busy if you really want to do it.

If you *do* make it back to a hotel, maybe just to talk further, here are a few icebreakers:

- Games. Strip anything will do. (Strip poker and strip blackjack are two good ones.)
- Spin the bottle is a really fun game and it helps to relieve tension.
- Music. Talk about or listen to.

Leave the TV off as it will divert everyone's attention from the real reason you're there. If you want to get things started that night, begin by making out with your partner. If the other couple is into it, they will respond in turn. And if they're playing games which allow you to take off your clothes, chances are, they will want to join in.

However, if the other couple just sits there like a bump on a log and doesn't do anything, they're not into it. Read their body language. Are they stiff? Have they avoided eye contact? Have they avoided personal contact with their partner? Look for the signs. If they're not into it, call it a night.

Keep in mind that if they are nervous or hesitant about getting a room, they're probably not going to be into it. You might be wasting your time with this couple.

If you're lucky, the other couple will start first.

Related experience:

Tabitha is one of the first swingers I met.

"Ed and I had been swinging for about a year. Well, to be truthful, we thought of ourselves as swingers even though we'd never actually *done* anything. We knew we would eventually but we all know it's hard to find the right couple.

We finally found them. We went out to dinner, then to a 'normal' club, then to a bar for drinks. We were out all night and having a great time but I'd already decided we weren't going to do anything because it was so late and all of us were tired.

As we left the bar, the other woman turned to me and said, 'We don't live far from here. How about you two follow us home and we'll have some more drinks there?'

We readily agreed and I thought we were just going to have drinks. Well, naïve me, a few drinks later, she and her husband started getting busy. They started to kiss and I mean kiss, as in suck-face. I could see their tongues going in and out of each other's mouths. I felt like such an idiot and I just sat there, my heart pounding. I was slightly uncomfortable and I have no problem admitting that. While I was aware of what went on, it was totally new to me and wasn't something I did everyday. I was new to it and so were they. But they seemed a lot more comfortable doing it than I did.

Ed turned to me and he started to kiss me. Soon, everyone was naked. It was weird. I kept thinking, 'Is this really happening?' I mean, I knew it was but it was almost surreal. It seemed to take forever for me to get wet. I was so nervous and I couldn't relax enough to get into it. I remember looking over at them a few times and just not believing they were having sex right next to us on the floor! She was on top of him and he glanced over at me. I tried to smile, but I couldn't get over the fact that I was having sex in front of another couple! We were really doing it!

I tried to get into it and concentrate on my pleasure, but I have to be honest and say I couldn't. I just wanted it to be over. I hate to say that because, later, swinging became something I was very comfortable with and enjoyed immensely, but at that moment, I just wanted it over.

They finished first and left the room for a little bit so we could finish up. It took a long time for Ed to come because he was as nervous as I was. Once we were done, I had to jump up and go to the bathroom. I had to have a minute to myself, to gain my bearings. My hands were shaking. I felt almost like I hadn't done it, but watched it or something. It was like my first time in a strip club, but amplified a thousand times.

I enjoyed it my first time but I was so nervous I didn't enjoy it as much as I thought I would. Now the second time we did it was hot. But that first time, I thought I would never get through it. I'm glad I did it, though because it led to a lot of great sex. But, damn it, that first time was hard as hell."

Usually, nervousness *does* play a key part in all of this. Just realize that you have to live through it to get to the better swinging experiences. It's almost like being a virgin all over again. You are a virgin to these new people; you are brand new to them. And you are brand new to yourself as well. You've never done anything like this. Why wouldn't you be nervous? *It's natural.*

And, like being a virgin, don't expect your first time to be stupendous. It may be awkward. It will make your heart pound and your hands shake. But so does riding a roller coaster. You're already there, so why not go ahead and go through with it and get it done? You can't get off a roller coaster during the middle of the ride, can you? You can leave the room during your first swing experience, but think about how you will feel afterwards. If you don't leave, you will be so proud of yourself for having the balls to do it.

Be assured after the first, the others will be easier. For some reason, the first swing experience is usually the hardest. No one really knows what to do. You might want to try to swing with an experienced swinger couple at first. They've been there, they've done that and to them, it's no big deal. They won't be as nervous as you and will be more likely to make the first move. Everyone knows you're there for sex, it's no secret. Don't allow yourself to become inhibited at the last minute. Taking that first step is hard, but be assured, it is well worth it.

If you find yourself with couple with no experience, just do what comes natural. There is really no way to tell you exactly what to do. Use your human instincts on this one. I think you will figure it out pretty easily.

Personal experience:
The first time we swung was scary. We'd met the couple previously and though nothing happened on our first date, we knew this was the one. They said they had been with another couple twice before, so that took the edge off somewhat.

We began the night with drinking and swapping life stories. Then we played a strip game and soon we were all naked. Next thing we did, since all of our clothes were off, was play spin the bottle and whomever the bottle pointed to, that person had to kiss. This was a great icebreaker. Soon, everyone was kissing everyone else—girls included, boys excluded—and we swapped right in front of each other. It was over in about fifteen minutes. We put on our clothes and had a drink, laughing at the silliness of it, but being so relieved it had gone okay.

Swinging, in a lot of ways, is play. It's very adult, but also has an underlying playful attitude to it. Sometimes it can get downright silly.

Related experience:
I met Chelsea through an internet ad.

"We had gotten a hotel room and were so nervous because it was the first time for both of us. I almost wanted to leave. But then the other woman suggested we warm up by getting in the bathtub together and showering. I was so anxious, I just didn't know if I could do it. But I know that life is all about taking risks, and I wanted to do this so bad, so I took my chances and stripped, hoping I looked good and was desirable to everyone.

We got into the bathtub but it was crowded because both of our guys are way over six feet tall. The other woman and I started soaping them up, and then we started soaping each other up. I remember lingering on her nipples and getting really excited *down there* when she responded to my touches.

Next thing I know, we pushed the boys out of the tub and went at it. We kissed and touched and had so much fun together! The boys were happy standing by watching us. We didn't do a full swap until later, but it was a great way to get acquainted."

Taking risks is part of life and if you want to swing, you will have to step up to the plate and find out what you're made of. Sometimes, it's hard because you make it hard. You can put too much into it, too much analysis that will keep you inhibited forever.

Someone told me once, "Yeah, the first time was harder than I ever imagined, but afterwards, I was like, 'What is the big fucking deal?' It's just sex! Why do we always put so much into sex? It's stupid! It's not like we were mainlining drugs or anything, we were just fucking. It changed my outlook on life, sure it did. I definitely stopped taking it so seriously. However, it really didn't change my life that much. I am glad I did it that first time because if I hadn't, I wouldn't be where I am now, which is having the time of my life. I'm having fun. But if anyone had told me how hard it was going to be to do it that first time... Hell, I would have still done it. A million times over!"

Swinging will open your mind. Once you do it, you'll realize it's really not that big a deal. You'll probably wonder why you put so much into it in the first place. I know I certainly did.

So, once you're there and ready to do it, do it. Allow things go where they naturally will. You might just want to do a soft swing that night. You might just make out with your partner. You might not want to have actual intercourse. Whatever happens is cool. Just relax and *enjoy it.* Know that the next time will be a lot easier.

Don't forget to pat yourself and your lover on the back after it's done.

I just can't do it!

You made a date and you broke it. Or you made it to the date and you circled the parking lot and backed out at the last minute, leaving the other couple to wonder what the hell happened to you. Or you actually went on the date but couldn't actually do anything. Now it's driving you insane.

You're probably taking all of this way too seriously. Swinging is fun. It really is and, once you get over that initial roadblock, it can lead to some of the best times of your life. Lots of couples dabble in swinging but never actually have sex with other people. No biggie! It may be the actual thought of knowing you *can* do it is what gets you going. Sometimes this is enough.

Taking the first step is the hardest. Keep in mind that you don't have to swing. But if you do want to swing, you might have to force yourself to do it that first time. It can be awkward having sex in front (or with) strangers. But this is what swinging is all about. If you find yourself continuing to cancel or back out at the last minute time and time again, this is a good sign you're not cut out to be a swinger. Don't beat yourself up over it.

It is a hard thing to do and that first time can be a little intimidating. So relax. And, again with feeling, remember that the Lifestyle isn't for everyone.

You've been stood up!

Those bastards! *How could they?!* You've just spent a small fortune on new clothes, you've rearranged your schedule so much to meet them that you'll never get it back in order and, in addition to that, you've driven a good distance to get there and, guess what? They are nowhere to be found. Yes, you are correct. You, my friend, have been stood up.

Bastards!

As in dating, this can and will happen. And it's just as annoying, if *not* more, being stood up as a couple than as a single.

Yeah, yeah, we all know there are many reasons why people stand other people up. In my honest opinion, none of them hold any weight. (Okay, I know some things can and will happen and if they do, fine. But most times people don't show because they changed their minds. Don't expect them to return your emails, either.)

I don't like it one bit and no other self-respecting person does either.

They made a date with you. They didn't bother to cancel it either. They let on like they were going to be there, didn't they? And now they're not going to show. No. I don't like this at all.

Personal experience:

We'd been exchanging emails with this couple for about a month and had the date set at a nice Mexican restaurant. It was about an hour drive from our home. We got ready and left right on schedule.

We made good time and got there early and decided to go in and have a margarita while we waited. We were seated and our drinks were served in no time flat.

Then we waited. And waited. An hour passed. The waiter began to give us annoyed looks. (He was probably thinking we were just there for the free salsa and chips.) We began to get agitated ourselves and started wondering where the hell they were.

We had their cell phone number. Never one to be stood up and take it lying down (no pun intended) I gave them a call. And the husband answered. He had some nerve.

I demanded to know in a voice that should have told him I was pretty pissed off, "Uh, we're waiting. Where are you?"

He said, oh, so casually, "We left late."

"How late?"

"About a couple of hours late."

They lived about two hours away from the restaurant. This was more than great. It was fan-fucking-tastic!

"Well," I said, trying to remain calm. "Why don't we just forget it this time?"

I didn't say, *Why don't we forget it all-together?* But that's what I meant.

"We'll be there," he said.

"When?" I asked and looked at my watch.

"We just left, so a couple of hours."

They expected us to wait a couple of hours on them, in addition to the time we'd already put in? Oh, I don't think so.

"Well," I began. "I don't—"

"Here, talk to my wife," he said.

What was wrong with talking to him? I didn't want to talk to his wife! I wanted to end the conversation *with him* and order some food. I was starving!

She got on the phone and snapped, "Yes?!"

Now I was glad they hadn't showed. Her attitude was of super bitch proportions. Funny how people can seem so nice in emails but in real life, they can seem...*not so nice.*

I said, "We're going to do this another time."

"Fine with me," she said and I just knew she was rolling her eyes.

"Okay. Bye."

I hung up without waiting for her to respond.

Needless to say, we didn't swing with them. Anyone who is that inconsiderate doesn't deserve to have me as a lover. Sorry. The thing is, they had our cell phone number and could have called us to tell us they were running late. They didn't. Why? Because they were assholes.

They may have been fighting. Who knows what their excuse was? I don't really care. When someone makes someone else wait, they don't deserve to meet good people.

Another thing: *Always be on time*. No one likes to wait. If you make a couple wait, don't expect them to be happy about it. You might have just missed a golden swing opportunity. Too bad for you. Also, if you're late, they might assume that you're standing *them* up.

And they don't want to hear your excuses when you are late. Don't patronize people by telling them you had to let out the dog, or you had to wash a load of laundry or your mother, brother, great aunt or whoever called just as you were running out the door. You should have let the answering machine pick it up. Just apologize and tell them it won't happen again. And, if does, you're toast with this couple. More than likely, they're not going to give you a third chance to redeem yourself.

Related experience:
Ellen told me this story after she'd had a few drinks.

"Every single fucking time! Every single time they were late. And it wasn't just a little late; it was a lot late, like thirty minutes to an hour late.

They kept telling us, 'We're always on time! I don't know why we're always late!'

I knew why. They were fighting before they got there, that's why. I could tell because I can pick up on body language pretty well. They would sneak glares to one another out of the corner of their eyes and sometimes she would be such a bitch, I'd want to slap her.

Needless to say, they didn't work out.

The last date I told my husband, 'If they are over twenty minutes late, we're leaving.'

He said, 'You're damn right we are.'

And they were over twenty minutes late. We don't know how long it took them to get there. We didn't stick around to find out."

Good for them. If people are going to do this to you, tell them to go jump in the lake. Your time is just as important as theirs. And if you're the one who's late, you better have a damn good excuse because next time you're late, you might find yourself dining alone.

Soft swing? Maybe to *begin* with.

Soft swinging is doing everything with another person but actual intercourse. Usually, at the last minute, people switch back to their original partner and have sex in front of the other couple. It can be fun, but I've always wondered why go to the trouble if you can't do it all? It's like asking your partner not to look at anyone. I actually heard a woman tell her husband at a party, "Honey, don't stare at her. It makes me uncomfortable."

WHAT!?

But some people enjoy soft swinging; some even *prefer* it, especially on a first date. Some couples only go for the touching or oral sex. And that's fine. It's up to you what you want out of it. There is no right and wrong. If you only want to soft swing, only soft swing. As long as you are in your comfort zone, you will have a good time.

Just be sure to let the other couple know this is all you want to do. Don't be surprised, however, if they cancel the date. You can always find another couple who prefers soft swinging.

Again, what you want to do is fine. There are no right and wrong ways to do it. But I can assure you, once you do a soft swing, you'll more than likely want to go all the way. It's just a natural progression.

Full swap.

A full swap is when both partners swap partners with another couple and have intercourse. They either have same room sex or separate room sex.

That's pretty much it.

Same room or separate room sex?

After you've found the right couple to swing with, one of the questions comes up is, *Should we do it in the same room or go separately?*

This is entirely up to you but it is my personal opinion that if you can't handle your partner going off to be alone with someone else, you can't really handle swinging. You might be worrying too much about what they're doing to really enjoy it yourself. Give each other space. I might also recommend that you ask your partner and the other couple before anything happens what their preferences are.

Many couples like same room because they enjoy seeing their partners in the throes of passion. I was once told by a beautiful woman, "I love to see how his body tenses up when he's about to come. It fascinates me to see him like that. It's the best part for me, knowing he's getting off."

Again, it's a personal choice but understand that many couples will want to swing in the same room and many won't. Respect others' wishes.

A few guidelines:
- Establish *before* you swing what you're going to do.
- Ask the other couple *before* what their preferences are.

Again, if you have more than five rules, you're probably not ready for swinging. Prepare to feel uncomfortable—at first. And remember, it will pass.

Related experience:

I was told this by a woman at a swing club.

"We've been swinging for about three years now and we're having a blast. I met this girl who's a stripper and we hit it off, so I invited her to a party. We were having a great time and had decided to swap with her and her husband, who was a really good looking guy. And he had a good personality and that's what we're there for, so we went for it. We're one of those couples who can do the same room sex or separate room sex, it doesn't really make a difference to us, but she preferred separate rooms. Which was cool.

So we made off and did our thing and she took off with my husband to one of the other bedrooms. I had a great orgasm and thought they should be about finished, so I went to find them. I always like to see my husband first thing afterwards to compare notes. We share everything, by the way. Anyway, I find their room and try to open the door. It's locked! Locked! Okay. Time to confess. I don't mind separate rooms, but doors being locked, doors keeping me away from my man, I can't stand! Oooh! That drives me crazy. I'm willing to share but they can't take him away from me! And that's the exact message she was sending. I know he didn't do it, either. But being a man getting ready to get laid, he's not going to argue the point. I know it's a little silly but it's my rule and I expect other people to honor that.

It's just plain weird. I mean, what if I wanted to go in there and join them?

I made such a fool of myself. I banged on the door and demanded to be let in and everyone is staring at me, wondering if I've lost my mind because I'm usually cool as a cucumber at parties. My husband opens the door and I demand to know why it's locked and he's on the defense, 'She did it! Not me!' Before I knew what I was doing, I turned on her and said, 'Don't you ever touch my husband again!' I grabbed his hand and we left. He later told me that he told her not to lock the damn door but she insisted because she didn't like to be interrupted and wanted him 'all to herself'. Bitch.

I don't guess that chick was as cool as I thought she was. End of story."

Okay then.

Point is, please be courteous of others' rules. If not, you may find yourself on the other side of that door. Not a place I'd like to be. Also know everyone has their pet peeves. Honor them even if they don't make a bit of sense to you. Your rules might not make much sense to them, either.

Keep in mind.

Just do your best. That means doing what's right for you. No matter what happens, be content with knowing that you did your best to give swinging a try. And nobody can take that away from you.

Swing clubs.

Unless you live in a metropolitan area, more than likely you are going to have to travel to go to a swing club.

Swing clubs will vary from state to state, city to city, country to country. We once went to one where everyone was dressed in Western wear. (No, it wasn't western theme night either, that was just the way these particular people dressed. Remember, in swinging, it takes *all* kinds.) Needless to say, we didn't stay very long.

Some clubs will be very nice and some will not. If you get a bad vibe, don't hesitate to leave.

I sincerely recommend going to a swing club before you actually go on a first date with another couple. It's a party/club atmosphere and usually quite dark and anonymous so it's easier to hang back and observe what's going on without being expected to participate or converse. You can kind of get a feel for the Lifestyle by doing this first.

What can you expect at a swing club? First of all, they may be located in an older building in a seedier part of town. The rent is lower at places like that and allows the owners to operate at lower costs. Many club owners are swingers themselves.

Some swing clubs expect you to join as a member. This is just a legal formality so that the establishment can say it's a private members only facility. They have a register that you will have to fill out. This is for legal purposes and they don't care if you give a fake name or address. (My suggestion is that you do.)

Other clubs, you just pay upon entering. Admission fees will vary so bring plenty of cash as they do not usually take checks or credit cards.

There is usually no alcohol served at these clubs. But most times, they do have a table set up with finger food and sodas.

You may or may not see a few security guards walking around, so be on your best behavior.

Opening times will vary, of course, but I've been to many that open around ten at night. My advice to you is to get there an hour or two after they open. You don't want to be the first couple there as that will only add to the anxiety you will be experiencing.

The first time into a swing club can be intimidating. After you've entered, take time to walk around and see what they have to offer. The ones I've been to have several different rooms with plenty of seating. There will always be a TV room and an adult video will be playing (usually it's looped). This is a good place to sit down and get your bearings after you're done with your tour.

There will be several "private" rooms with small beds or mats and doors for privacy. If a door is closed, I wouldn't recommend opening it. You just might interrupt someone getting their brains fucked out. If people want you to watch, they will leave the door open.

There might also be some BDSM rooms and occasionally glory holes. There may be a dance floor and the music is usually very loud.

Most clubs have websites. Check a few out and don't be afraid to email the owners if you have questions. The worse thing that could happen is they don't email back.

Be sure to take time to stay a little while no matter how nervous you are. You paid good money to get into this club and if you stick around long enough, someone might come through that door that will make up for the nervous waiting time you've endured.

And if they don't? They don't. If you liked the club, you can come back at a later date to try again, or you can find a new one to go to next time.

Sometimes, a swinger couple will decide to branch out on their own and start a club by hosting it in a hotel or maybe at their house. There is an entrance fee and sometimes a membership fee in addition to the entrance fee.

Personal experience:

During our second year of swinging, we were contacted by the hostess of a party we'd attended on New Year's. She was starting her own club and was planning to host parties on a monthly basis. The membership fee was twenty-five dollars. We'd had a great time at her party, so we decided to join and sent her the money through the mail. We waited and waited for any news of the club opening but there never was any. We got one email informing us that they had a lot of things going on and would resume the club as soon as possible. *As soon as possible* turned out to be never and we lost the money.

It wasn't a lot of money, but it was a bad way to do business. Because of this, I never pay for a club membership before attending. And if anyone asks for it in advance before I am at the club, I find another club to attend.

But be your own judge. These things have a tendency to come and go pretty quickly, so if you get an opportunity to attend, go for it. It might not be there next time you want to go.

Swing parties.

Double-headed dildos. Nudity. Silly games. Finger foods. Feeling up. Kissing strangers. Dirty jokes.

These are the basics of a swing party. They are usually private, invite-only gatherings held at private residences or hotel suites. As with everything in swinging there is no hard and fast rule. There is usually a per couple entrance fee. If you plan on partying late into the night, it might be wise to book a room for yourself somewhere close so you won't have to drive. (*Do not ever drink and drive!*) And always be prepared. Have condoms on hand. You might just get lucky.

But how do you get invited to a swing party? Good question.

An internet swingers club is the best way. We were once invited to join a club through our internet ad but most times, we just find them ourselves. When you find the club you want to join, you have to apply. After you apply, you might be screened. And by this I mean, you might be asked to send a picture of both of you and answer some questions. Don't get scared. Most of the questions are simple ones like, "What brought you to the Lifestyle?" and "How old are you?" There is a possibility that you might have to have a face-to-face meeting with the club's organizers as well.

You could hear about a party through word of mouth from other swingers. If you stay in the Lifestyle long enough, you will meet plenty of people who will invite you to parties.

Whatever way you get there is fine, though, just as long as you get to go.

Related experience:
My friend, Tammy, told me this story.

"It was only our second party and we left late. It was about an hour and half drive and we were so scattered we forgot to bring the directions. Of course, we didn't realize this until we were half-way there. But I figured we'd get there and look the hosts up in the phonebook, get the directions and go on over. We got there, found a phone booth (I didn't have a cell phone then) and called information. Their number was unlisted! But, for some reason, I thought I knew the general direction of the house because I had read the directions beforehand. I thought we'd know it was the right house because all these cars would be parked out front. We drove and drove and drove. By this time, we were fighting because we were so frustrated. We never found that damn house and I was really upset because the hostess was a good friend of mine. I think she thought I'd stood her up even though I told her what had happened. I've always felt bad over it, too."

The moral of this story? Plan, plan, plan. Be sure to print out directions and phone numbers. And be sure to give yourself plenty of time to get there so you won't be rushed.

Another thing to keep in mind is that you won't be the only couple there for the first time. This also applies to swing clubs. So when you go, don't hesitate to talk to other people.

Related experience:

Jan told me this story after we met at a swing party.

"Anyway, it was our first time to a swing party. I had no idea what to expect. My husband and I were very nervous. The party was held in a hotel suite. We went right up to the door and knocked. We were let in and the whole place was packed. I felt like such a dork because I hadn't dressed as sexy as some of the other women.

Because it was our first time, we kind of hung around the back of the room. It's so hard to talk to people in these kinds of situations, isn't it? I know it was hard for me.

The music was very loud and some women were dancing together. The men just stood back and watched. They had a refrigerator stocked full of drinks and beer, so I had a couple of beers and finally got the courage up to talk. I approached a very attractive woman who appeared to be in her early thirties. I introduced myself and said, 'This is our first time.'

She smiled at me and my husband and said, 'Mine too!'

I couldn't believe it. I asked, 'You've never been to a swing party?'

She cracked up and said, 'No, I mean, it's my first time to *this* party.'

I was so embarrassed. But she assured me that even if no one else would admit to it, there were a lot of new people there. I was glad at our next party that we weren't new anymore, though."

The first one is always the hardest. Always. Just remember to relax and enjoy yourself.

Do you want to host your own party?

After this story, you might not.

Related experience:
This is Jill's story.

"We'd been swinging for a few years and were having a blast doing it. In fact, it was one of the best decisions we'd ever made as a couple. But we were spending a lot of money to do it, what with hotels and club fees. I got this crazy idea to host a party and maybe make a little money to help with future swinging expenses. It took a lot of planning, to say the least, and a lot of time. I emailed everyone I knew in the Lifestyle, set the date, bought the food and because I was having it at my house, I served some drinks. Well, the party was set to start at seven and that's early, I know, but I think most parties get started way too late. Seven came and went, then eight. A few couples came. By nine we had about ten people total there. Not many. We had a good time, but I went in the hole financially. It wasn't worth it. Some people might make money hosting parties, but I didn't. And, get this, my house got trashed. Never again."

I have this saying: *A party is always a lot more fun at someone else's house.*

But it's your decision. Take care with it. If you're planning on making some money with parties, you need to plan it all out in advance and make sure you cover your costs.

Free for all? I don't think so.

One thing that I should mention is that a lot of people go to parties and clubs or even on dates thinking it's a free-for-all. It's not.

When you go to an event more than likely you will see all kinds of crazy stuff going on. However, you can't just jump in there and do as your like nor can you stick things places where they are not invited. You have to be *specifically invited* to join in on the fun. It might be a casual tilt of the head or a nod, but if you don't get it, *keep your distance.*

Related experience:

I've known Jackie forever.

"Well, how do I put this politely? I don't think I can. I like gangbangs. There, I said it. I like gangbangs. Three or four good looking guys all around me touching me all over and doing all kinds of other stuff I love. I know it's not everyone's cup of tea, but, hell, it's mine! And that's all that matters.

Anyway, this is almost funny. My boyfriend and I were at this very large club in a very large city. The night was going pretty good and we got some guys together for a good old fashioned gangbang. We took one of the back rooms without a door because that's all that was left at that point. I usually like a door because I like to control who's in the room. Also, I don't like to be interrupted and I hate looking up with some guy's dick in my mouth to see other people staring at me. I might like gangbangs, but I don't like voyeurs. Go figure.

So, I've got three guys that night and my boyfriend, who usually is just there to make sure no one gets rough with me. (He also instructs them on what to do. 'You go there, you do this.') He does participate occasionally but he likes to see it; sometimes he even videotapes me and we watch it later and it is hot!

So, there, I've got my boys and I am having a good time and all of a sudden I notice there is more than three of them. There's like, five! My three boys and two others I didn't invite.

To say the least, I was not happy about this. If I don't invite you, you don't attend. I handpick my guys.

I asked these dudes, 'What are you doing in here?'

They just stood there like a bunch of dweebs. One of them finally pointed to the door and said, 'It was open.'

I was like, 'Open? There isn't even a door!'

He was like, 'Uh…uh…'

I told him and his buddy, 'Get the fuck out of my gangbang!'

And what happened, you ask? They got the fuck out of my gangbang. I never use those rooms anymore. Either it's got a door or it doesn't happen. End of discussion."

Okay then. End of discussion.

Off and on-premise. What are they?

Simply put, an on-premise party means people will be having sex on the party site, whether it's a hotel room, someone's house, or a club. Off-premise means that if you hook up with someone, you have to take it somewhere else.

What to expect at parties and clubs.

- Gangbangs (usually one woman and several guys on a bed going at it.)
- Glory holes.
- A stranger copping a feel of you or your partner.
- A stranger kissing you or your partner.
- All kinds of people from all different walks of life.
- Loud music.
- A designated smoking area.
- Girls with girls.
- Lots of people walking around naked.
- Slutty clothes.
- People having sex all over the place.

Remember, don't stand in the corner and wait for someone to come to you. Get out there and have fun! Everyone knows why you're there. And don't be offended if a stranger sticks their hands down the back of your pants. It's happened to me a lot. It's fun.

Important tip:

One of the most important things to remember in swinging is to just be yourself. If you pretend to be something you're not, you might just forget who you are. And other people will soon catch on.

What not to do when at parties, clubs and on dates.

- Don't be pushy! No one likes it and it will get you labeled.
- Don't brag about how much money you have, how big your penis is or anything else. DON'T BRAG!
- Don't lie about your swing experiences. This will only come back to bite you in the ass. If you want to share, fine, but don't embellish too much.
- Don't offer information about your past swinging experiences if you haven't swung a lot unless specifically asked. Some people might take it the wrong way and think you're not ready to party. If asked, don't lie, though. And change the subject if it makes you uncomfortable.
- Don't give personal information out freely. Just because you're having sex with these people doesn't mean they have to know your whole history.
- Don't try too hard to be *too* funny or sexy. Everyone is as nervous as you even if they don't show it.
- Don't hound someone thinking you might get lucky with them. Do not try to "keep" them all to yourself. No, no, no.

- Don't drink too much.
- Don't be loud or obnoxious.
- If someone has turned you down, move on and DO NOT follow them around the room hoping they'll change their minds. They won't and you'll be labeled a creep.
- Don't pretend to be something you're not. Be yourself. Everyone likes an individual.
- Don't load up on heavy meals before an event. Because you already have butterflies in your belly, they will usually sit like a rock in your stomach and make you miserable.
- Don't forget to bring condoms. *EVER.* (Even if the hosts have supplied the condoms, I always bring my own because they are usually in a big bowl in plain site of everyone. I am paranoid about someone doing something to them.)
- Always remember: *Better safe than sorry.* If you have a bad feeling about someone, move away from them.

What to do at clubs, parties and on dates.

Things to do:

- Be polite.
- Listen to what others are saying. You just might learn something.
- Don't hesitate to ask questions of the host. They are usually happy to help, especially people that are new to swinging.
- Mingle, mingle mingle. You're there to meet new people.
- Take a chance. You never know what will happen.
- Stand back and take it all in. It's pretty cool, isn't it?
- HAVE FUN!

No means no!

Any good swinger takes the first "no" and moves on with no hard feelings. If you don't want to play, don't play. And if you're the one who's been turned down, *do not* make someone uncomfortable by hounding them.

On average, it's usually men who won't take "no" for an answer. If you're a woman and have been approached by someone and you don't want to do anything with them, simply decline and move on. If they won't leave you alone, ask your partner to tell them to leave you alone. If they still insist, notify the management and more than likely, they will kick the guy out.

Don't hesitate to do it. Some guys can be overly aggressive and won't take no for an answer even when they should. Do not jeopardize yourself by being a "nice" person. If you're not interested, you're not interested.

Personal experience:

I was once at a large swing club in a big city. The place was crowded and I was at the bar sipping a soda when a couple sat down next to me. My partner had gotten up to do a little wandering on his own. This is cool. We do it all the time.

We conversed nicely for a few minutes and then the guy invited me to join them in a threesome. To be polite, they were not my type at all, so I politely turned them down. The guy got somewhat pissed off and kept at me, asking me over and over to have sex with them. His girlfriend just sat there with this dumb smile on her face. Again, I declined. He said some pretty rude things to me then about how I must be really uptight and an experience like this would really loosen me up.

Because I was so new to swinging, I thought for some reason I had to sit there and listen to him subtly berate me. I got very lucky then. Another couple who had overheard him came over and sat next to me and started talking, essentially rescuing me from this guy. I was very grateful to them. They later told me I didn't have to put up with that and should have gotten up and left.

This all took place in about the course of five minutes, maybe less. That's how aggressive this guy was. He had his fantasy and my "uptight" behavior was not going to stand in the way of his fantasy. Maybe I felt bad for them because they weren't all that attractive. I just felt I *had* to be nice and being nice at a swing club can cost you a lot of time that you *could* be spending looking for someone you're attracted to. I don't know what it was with me that night, but I can assure you, I'd never do that again. I would never sit there and take that shit from anyone now. And my suggestion to you is start off with this attitude.

Keep in mind, when these kinds of things happen, you will usually be by yourself. Your partner may have stepped out of the room for a cigarette or bathroom break. These aggressive people pick women sitting alone because they know they're more vulnerable. My advice is to hang around other couples you're attracted to until you get your bearings.

I know we're all there to socialize and there is nothing wrong with being friendly and polite. However, sometimes it gives off the wrong message. Some people go into swinging thinking that everyone will want to do them simply because they're *there*. *We* might not be desperate to get laid, but *they* are.

Something else to consider. If you meet a couple and find yourself physically attracted to only one of them, it's probably not going to work out. The other couple may become pushy and make the situation uncomfortable. They might even try to talk you into doing something you really don't want to do by making you feel guilty. I've heard this a million times, "You're here, why not do it?"

Why not? Because you don't want to do it with them, that's why.

If you are uncomfortable, remove yourself from the situation. Your partner should follow suit. My rule is we both play or neither of us plays. That way, there are no fights to deal with later. Your partner should be that considerate of you.

If your partner's the one who is uncomfortable with the situation, have consideration for him/her and don't try to talk them into doing something they don't want to. They might tell you to do whatever you like and enjoy yourself, but chances are they really want you with them. If someone is making them *that* uncomfortable, something is amiss. If they have to leave the room to get away from these people, these people might be bad news.

Related experience:
This comes from Jack.

"We were involved with this couple. My wife really wasn't into the guy but told me I could play, have a threesome or something. The guy must have had his feelings hurt because my wife didn't want anything to do with him so he kept pestering her. She left the room at one point, but told me I could stay. I stayed and we did a little threesome action. But it didn't feel right with her not being there."

If it doesn't feel right, do yourself a favor and don't do it. And always remember, you are in this together.

Group sex.

We all know what group sex is, don't we? It's when more than two people hook up at a party or a club and go at it together, in a group. There are hands, lips, breasts and dicks everywhere. Everyone is touching everyone else everywhere. (The men typically don't do anything with one another.)

Group sex is great. It can be a lot of fun for all involved. It's an intense sexual experience. But sometimes it happens when you don't necessarily want it to.

Personal experience:
It was the second time I'd been to this party and the first time I was there, I lusted after one particular guy. He was just my type. We didn't get to hook up the first night because of extenuating circumstances. (Girl/girl/girl threesome.)

So when I saw him there the next time, I was overjoyed. We flirted a little and then he went one way and I went the other. Soon, it was getting late and I found myself in the smoking room about to fall asleep in a chair. My husband came in and told me that things were getting wild in the other room and I should come have a look.

I was in.

I woke up in a hurry and followed him into the living room. It was getting pretty wild. In fact, I was the only person in there with any clothes on. (My pants. My shirt had disappeared hours earlier.) Everyone was naked and dancing and kissing and feeling and touching. I saw one of my friends giving a blow job to some guy. Then I saw the object of my lust and he grinned at me. I went over to him and my partner took up with a girl he'd met earlier.

It didn't take a second for us to start kissing. I think we both said "Hi" and then went at it. Since he was already naked, he helped me out of the remainder of my clothes and walked me over to the couch, where we find a spot for ourselves.

We're all over each other and are pretty much ignoring everyone else. They can do what they want to, but we just wanted each other at that moment.

Next thing I know, this guy who I did not find all that desirable had his dick in my face. Since I'm a little drunk, I think, "Sure, why not?" and gave him a little head. Then it occurred to me that this was not the guy I was here to fuck. I was also a little taken aback and thought, *"Who invited you?"*

So, I moved away from him and go back to my lust partner who, at that moment, was receiving a blowjob from the guy's wife.

He looked up at me and threw his hands up, *"Who invited her?"* I didn't want to be a bitch and tell her to get his dick out of her mouth, so, I moved over towards her, pulled her head back and kissed her neck, hoping to slowly but politely move her away from my guy. (I mean, he was the reason I came back to this party and I wanted to do him!)

She responded and she and I kissed a little, but then she went back to his dick. Then her husband is all over me, kissing me and the next thing I know, he's giving me head. I'm like, *"Whatever."*

Me and the guy glanced at each other as if to say, *"What the fuck?!"* Well, if someone is going to give me head, I'm going to let them. I laid there for a minute, getting into it.

Then my guy began to kiss me. I removed my crotch from the other guy's face, pushed him out of the way and jumped up. Me and my guy rushed into one of the bedrooms, found a secluded spot and had some wild sex.

End of story.

I guess the point is, when you're in a group session, most people assume, rightly so, that's it a free for all. If you don't want to attend, just get up like we did and move to a more private area. But if you do want to go for it, go for it. If someone doesn't want to kiss you, they won't. But more than likely, if you find yourself in a love group, you are going to get lucky.

Don't forget the condoms!!

Open relationships.

Perhaps you're reading this book and the idea of swinging isn't exactly what interests you. Yet you still want to experience sex with other people. What you might be looking for is an open relationship, which simply means that you and your partner have an agreement to have sex with other people but not necessarily in a swinging situation.

Sex on the side, if you will.

It's your choice. This is cool. Lots of couples have this agreement. In fact, many couples have agreements to be swingers and have an open relationship at the same time. You never know when you might meet someone and want an afternoon filled with lust.

Keep in mind that, along with swinging, open relationships require a lot of trust. Sometimes they require even more trust because the sex is taking place outside of the relationship. They don't know exactly what you're doing and you don't know exactly what they're doing. You will still need to set up a few rules and guidelines. And, of course, *always* be careful.

One of the most negative aspects of this sort of relationship is the fact that you're not doing it together. You are, in fact, picking up another person, taking them to a hotel or wherever and fucking them. That other person may develop a crush on you and make your life a living hell. Dealing with people in this way requires tact. While it's not necessary to fully explain your situation to them about what you and your partner are doing, some honesty *is* required. In swinging, no one really asks you what you're doing there. They know you're there to get fucked. They know because they're there for the same reason. When you go out and one-on-one with someone who is, more than likely, not a swinger, there may be consequences to pay. Ask yourself if it's worth it.

Related experience:

This is Al's story.

"Mary and I had agreed to do this open relationship thing. She'd go out with her friends and party but I wasn't that into it, so at first, I stayed home. Well, I got sick of that real quick and found myself in a bar, being hit on by a beautiful woman. We hit it off and decided to go get a room somewhere and had a really good time fucking. I went home and told Mary and she got kind of upset, like she didn't think I'd ever do it, even though she was doing it every weekend. Anyway, it gets worse.

I was really upset with Mary and went back to the same bar and the woman I fucked was there, so I thought, *Why not do it again?* We had another really great time, and then she asks for my number and told me I should sleep over. She said, 'We've got the room for the entire night. Why don't you stay?' Well, because my wife might kill me if I did.

I decided to come clean with her. I told her my situation and that I was married. She freaked out and told me I was using her. I told her I thought she understood what I was about. I had my wedding ring on for God's sake! But she wouldn't listen and stormed out of the room in tears. But what could I do? I had no interest in pursuing this woman because I had a really great one at home.

She was looking for a husband and I was only looking to get laid. Mary and I have since reconsidered our open relationship and have decided to lay off it for a while. I'd like to do it more because it was fun. I just didn't expect all this emotional stuff. Maybe we'll try it again in a few years. I hope so. It turned a little sour, but during it was really nice."

Those are good words to live by. You can stop and try again later. Give yourself permission to make mistakes, but always be upfront and honest with others to avoid hurting feelings.

Swingers don't really have to hide who they are when they're around other swingers. So, to me anyway, this is a more conducive lifestyle choice. And swingers don't have to worry about taking their wedding rings off, nor do they have to worry about lying to another person about their reasons for getting laid. They're getting laid because they're free to do so. Not everyone has this open-mindedness about relationships and sometimes, people can be downright mean about it.

Related experience:

This is Janet's story.

"Bob and I had agreed to an open relationship and I was itching to get started. I went to a bar alone—stupid, I know!—and this guy hit on me. He was nice looking and I allowed him to buy me a drink. After a while, I'm feeling it and ask him if he'd like to…you know. And he agreed, but then he asked if I was married. I told him that I was. I mean, why not? I was, thinking about how cool my husband was to go through with something like this. He asked me if my husband knew where I was and I offhandedly said, *Of course, he knows!* He was like, *Doesn't he mind?* I said no and told him about our arrangement and the guy just freaked out on me, telling me I was a slut and my husband was a weirdo to let his wife out like that. He said all this crap, really hurting my feelings. I left the bar in tears.

Later on, I gave it another shot just because I wasn't going to let that asshole get the best of me. I didn't inform the next guy I picked up about my lifestyle choice. I mean, why should I? I just fucked him and left. And I never give them my number."

People have different opinions about these kinds of non-traditional relationships. Don't let other people's preconceived notions keep you from doing what you want to do, but do be aware that not everyone is going to agree with your lifestyle choice.

Another thing to remember, an agreement is mutual consent between you and your partner. That doesn't mean as long as you don't get caught it's cool to do it. You have to actually be able to tell your partner about it after it's done. Maybe even a quick call beforehand wouldn't be bad. I mean, if you have an agreement, they're not going to tell you can't do it, are they?

And as long as you feel safe with this stranger. And that's what they are. They're strangers. You do not know these people nor do you know what they're capable of. Use your instincts. If you get a bad vibe, walk away. There is an enormous risk involved in this and you should be very aware of it. You don't want to get hurt.

Personal experience:

I was barhopping with a few girlfriends one night when I met this cute man who was a little younger than me. We boogied on the dance floor and had a great time conversing. When he asked me about my wedding ring, I told him that I was married, but gave off signals that it was cool that he could keep talking to me. A little later, he walked me to my car and we kissed. It was a nice, sweet kiss and he wanted me to go home with him.

I was very tempted but it was late. I also thought of my husband, who was at home, so I declined. Another thing, I didn't feel one-hundred percent comfortable with this guy. There was just something a little off about him. I couldn't put my finger on it, but I backed away.

I went home and told my husband about my night. He told he was glad I didn't hook up with the guy because he's always afraid someone might hurt me. He always says, "You can never be too careful."

And that's one reason we chose swinging. So we can do it together. Also, because he wants to keep an eye out for my safety.

Related experience:

The same night, one of my girlfriends hooked up with a guy, took *him* home and had some mind-blowing sex. He left the next morning and they haven't seen each other since.

So, it can work both ways. If this is something you want to do, go to a hotel. *Be seen.* Tell someone what you are doing and where you are going and introduce the person to your friends. Never leave without informing someone where you are going. It might take a little of the fun out, but as my partner says, "You can never be too careful."

And you can't.

When an affair turns into something else.

It happens. It really does. You and your partner have begun to adventure of a lifetime and each of you is getting something great out of it. Your sex life is better because of it. You're better because of it.

Then, you meet someone else. You have sex with them and you feel something a little more than lust. A casual encounter suddenly turns into something else entirely. And if you're relishing it and keeping it from your partner, it's more than a successful swing experience. It's an affair. It may be fun, but consider your partner. If you know you still love them, I would suggest you *BREAK IT OFF*. And if you don't, then it's time to confess. Don't make your partner a victim. You wouldn't want it done to you, would you?

Related experience:

I have this friend who had an affair. She never told me if she and her husband had an agreement but I gathered that they did. She started the affair with just sex in mind. Because he was a single guy, he wanted her to leave her husband. She told him, "Not going to happen. He gives me everything I need." They continued to see each other for *years*, occasionally taking breaks. He finally stopped asking her to leave her husband and after that, they stopped seeing each other.

She made her choice. She loved her husband more than she loved the sex. She says she made the right choice but, "It was fun while it lasted." Tell that to the guy whose heart she broke.

Enough said.

Something to consider.

The more fun you have, the more fun everyone else will have. Be the first to do something wild and crazy and bring the crowd along with you. Parties are usually loud, so get in the middle of the dance floor and boogie. If you're a woman, be the first one to take your top off. Be assured, many more will follow.

If you're at a club, go up and talk to a good looking stranger. Smile a lot. People are always attracted to nice smiles.

What will the neighbors think?

Who cares?! Let them think what they want to think. Do what feels good *for you.*

Voyeurs.

If you're only into this to watch, be warned that some swingers do not like voyeurs. It's not polite to stare at sexual activity unless you have been *specifically invited*. A glance or two is fine, but outright gawking is downright creepy.

Personal experience:
I once attended a party that got pretty wild. Everyone was walking around naked and I hooked up with a great guy while my partner took off into a bedroom with the guy's wife. While I was having fun, I kept noticing this couple (who were not naked) standing in the corner watching us. We kept at it for about twenty minutes and they never took their eyes off us. Because of this, I couldn't relax and really enjoy myself. Every time I'd look up, they'd be there with their mouths hanging open.

To say the least, it creeped me out.

Now some people love for others to watch but it is my recommendation that if you are being watched and you don't like it, move away from the watchers. If you find yourself watching, make a note to look somewhere else unless you are invited to watch. You might get lucky and even be invited to participate.

Swingers who want people to watch will usually leave the door open on the room they're swinging in. People in group areas sometimes get carried away and while they don't mind having sex in a room full of people, they might not necessarily like to be stared at.

As far as staring at people, the same rules apply in a swing party as do in the real world. If you persist in watching without invitation, you will more than likely be labeled a creep and no one wants to be labeled a creep in the Lifestyle. We're all there to have a good time. *Be considerate.*

Ken and Barbie.

Many couples go to swing events expecting to see Ken and Barbie, a beautiful supermodel-type couple who will fulfill all their desires and fantasies. The only problem with this is that Ken and Barbie do not attend swing parties; in fact they are sitting on a shelf in a toy store somewhere. Ken and Barbie aren't real!

Let's face it. We all want the Ken and Barbie couple. We all want to be with the more attractive people. But as I've said, Ken and Barbie don't exist, though there are sometimes very good looking couples in the Lifestyle. While this in and of itself is not a rarity, keep in mind that most swingers are normal people, not models. Everyone has a few stretch marks or pimples and even cellulite. This is because swingers are people, *real* people and real people are in no way perfect.

You might want to consider this: The better looking couples have just as many issues, if not more, as anyone else and sometimes they are not worth the trouble of dealing with because most extraordinary looking people also have extraordinary egos.

Personal experience:
We knew this couple who attended the same parties as we did. While they were good looking, they were no in any way, shape or form, Ken and Barbie. However, they thought they were.

They had huge egos and would scope the room almost with disdain. If someone not as "attractive" as them would approach them, they wouldn't give them the time of day.

And I didn't give them the time of day, either. I don't like pretension. I don't care for ego. We're all there to have a good time. To me, it's not about whose better looking than someone else. It's about who's fun.

One night, the guy must have set his eye on me. I didn't want to anything to do with him. And, as he would stare at me, he had this sly smile on his lips as if he almost thought he was giving me a big compliment by just *looking* at me.

I didn't look back and ignored him most of the night.

Well, later on, he finally made his move. And I decided to give him a try. (Maybe I was a little drunk. I don't know.) I mean, why not? I was at a swing party and that's why you go, isn't it?

Besides, I wanted to know what it would be like to fuck someone with that big of an ego.

I'll tell you what it's like. You're not fucking them, they're fucking you. It was about his dick and his lips and his everything. I kicked my own ass for allowing him to touch me. It was one of the worse fucks I'd ever had.

And, get this. After he was done he had the nerve to say, "Bet you're glad you finally got me."

Yes, I was mortified and promised myself I would never talk to him ever again. I've kept my promise.

Someone doesn't have to be traditionally good looking to have fun with. But you should be attracted to something about them. Right? If the attraction isn't there, why do it? And in order to have a good time, all it usually requires is mutual attraction, on a physical and/or mental level.

So forget about finding Ken and Barbie. They're not cool enough to be swingers.

Something to think about.

Note: You are there to have a good time. Don't get hung up on swinging with one particular person. If people don't want anything to do with you, move on. It is their loss.

Precautions.

Condoms, condoms, condoms. Preferably with spermacide.

Don't let people's good looking exterior fool you. Sexually transmitted diseases and pregnancy are risks involved with swinging. *Be smart.* Remember, you don't know this person that well and you certainly don't know their sexual history. You don't know where or with whom they've been with. You don't know what they're going to do. Always use precaution even if they tell you you don't have to.

Personal experience:

I was once at a party and had sex with a guy. He was nice, cute and affable. After we started, he kept asking me if he could come on my stomach. I kept telling him no because you never know when something can happen. I mean, I barely knew this guy's name, much less his sexual history or how many women he had been with. To be safe, I always insist they keep a condom on *at all times.*

We had been getting it on pretty heavily and I'm about to come when the next thing I know, he was coming all over my stomach. Reality kicked me in the ass. Oh, my God, I thought, what has he done?!

I got so mad at him and hissed, "I told you not to do that!"

He kept assuring me it was no big deal. Well, maybe not to him it wasn't.

I went into the bathroom and washed off. I spent the next month worrying about whether or not I was pregnant or had some kind of disease. You see, I didn't know *when* he took that condom off. For all I know, he never even had it on.

Just be smart and don't let this happen to you. Luckily, I wasn't pregnant or had any diseases and I *never* let this happen again.

Sometimes, you can't trust that people will do the right thing. When you hook up with someone at a party or a club, they are basically strangers to you. You don't know their backgrounds or where they came from. They can be unpredictable. For all you know, they come from rough backgrounds and have prison records. This isn't always the case, but it *can* happen. Be aware of it. You don't want to find yourself on the receiving end of someone else's unpredictability.

Things can get complicated, especially if you're a woman. Like I've said before, you don't know these people that well. And when you're at a party, things can get out of hand due to excessive drinking or just because you've decided to let loose and enjoy yourself. There are people out there who will take advantage of it. They're just looking for their opportunity to strike.

And if you ever hear these words, "I don't like to use a condom!" tell them to fuck off and move away from them. Remember, it's *you* that will have to pay the consequences, not them.

So, therefore, *safe sex is good sex* and it's the only kind of sex to have.

Oh, yeah, if you don't know anything about sexually transmitted diseases or how women get pregnant, you might not be ready for swinging.

Getting in shape for swinging.

It is necessary to look your best. The better shape you're in, the more likely you're going to hook up. Swinging is a form of dating and you want to impress. And you will have a better chance of getting laid if you look good.

It doesn't take that much. Cut your calories. I was at one time about thirty pounds overweight. What prompted me to lose weight was a good look in the mirror. I couldn't believe how much weight I'd gained since I'd gotten married! I had just slipped into this comfortable life and ate whatever I wanted, whenever I wanted.

Then one day, I walked past a mirror and caught a glimpse of myself out of the corner of my eye. I said to myself, "Who's that fatass?" Then, of course, I realized that fatass was me and that I had to do something about my weight.

When I first started losing weight, I would cut my meals in half. I'd have what I wanted, but only *half* of it. My tips are simple. I never eat at night and I never snack. I also exercise four times a week. When I first started working out, I couldn't even do a "girl" pushup. I can proudly say that I can now do thirty "boy" pushups. Being strong is a great feeling.

Start working out. A simple jog can do wonders. You do not have to invest in expensive (and rarely used after purchase) exercise equipment. Free weights are relatively inexpensive and there are many simple exercises you can do with them to get in shape. You can get lots of exercise ideas from fitness magazines and on the web. Do a little research and fit it into your schedule. Everyone has at least twenty to thirty minutes a day to exercise.

The biggest problem is that most people don't make it a priority. If you want to be a swinger, make it a priority. Give yourself time to do it. You work hard and you deserve it. *Don't look at it as a punishment.* Look at it as a way to make yourself look and feel better. And you will look and feel better once you start.

There are no secrets to weight loss. It's all pretty straightforward stuff. Exercising and cutting calories are the biggies.

Once you've gotten into shape, reward yourself by buying new clothes. *Prepare* yourself for your swinging experiences. The better you look, the better you will feel. Looking good will give you confidence.

You, yourself, know that people who are in good shape are more physically attractive. Be one of those people that everyone wants to have fun with.

Clothes make the man. And the woman. But especially the man.

Someone once said this to me at a club, "He *could* be cute if he wasn't dressed like he was on his way to a baseball game."

It's true. The better you dress, the more likely you will hook up. You want to look hot and that includes wearing stylish clothes.

I don't know why it is, but these days everyone seems to dress like they just don't give a shit about how they look. If you look back at the fifties and sixties and even seventies, when people went out, they dressed up and looked their best. Even if they were just going to the grocery store. Now people don't care. This is all well and good in everyday life, but if you want to be a successful swinger, you are going to have to take the time and money to look your best.

Clothes are not that expensive and they are a good investment. You can find great clothes at outlet malls and sometimes at consignment shops. If you have an outfit that's over two years old, it might be a good idea to leave it in the closest.

You want to look stylish. I've seen lots of nice looking people who just don't have a clue as to how to dress. They don't usually hook up at parties (at least not until everyone is naked.) It might not be "fair" but that's how it really is. Other people are too nice to come out and tell you they didn't want to fuck you because you weren't dressed nice. But then again, they won't fuck you either. You don't want to jeopardize your chances of getting lucky because you were dressed like a dork.

Sometimes, all people will give you is *one glance.* That first impression is very important. If they don't like what they see, they are not going to give you the time of day. Sad but true, especially in swinging. People want to fuck other people who look good. You don't have to be a supermodel to get laid, but it is important to wear clothes that tell people what kind of person you are. If you look like a million bucks, everyone is going to want to know who you are. And they're probably going to want to fuck you as well.

For some reason, men always seem to have the biggest problem dressing. Just go out and buy yourself a nice, solid color shirt and pair of nice black slacks and pair it with a nice pair of real leather shoes. This is always a good outfit and if you have good pec muscles, this kind of shirt will show the ladies how good they are.

Note: A golf shirt is *not* a good shirt to wear. It is not a good indicator that you have any style whatsoever. Never, ever wear a shirt with your favor team's logo on it. I don't care how big a fan you are or if they just won the superbowl, don't do it. Please.

Also, *NO BALL CAPS!* No. Just *don't* do it. You are not going to Hooters here. You are going out to present yourself for fucking.

You want to look hip and stylish but never (NEVER!) sleazy. NO gold chains and if you must wear an earring, a small hoop or stud is fine.

One of the first things people will look at is your shoes. I don't know why this is, but you can tell so much about a person by just looking at their shoes. Nice, leather shoes in a classic style are the best for men. (These kinds of shoes usually do not have hiking boot bottoms. Nor are they hiking boots.) You don't have to buy five or six pairs, just one good pair to keep for your dates and nights out at the club.

Don't wear Sebago's or dock shoes as they went out of style about twenty years ago. And if you have a pair of Sebago's, please do the rest of the world a favor and throw them out. I, surely, don't have to mention that you should not wear tennis shoes. Right?

Don't wear shoes that have the flap hanging off or are torn and dirty.

One more thing: Underwear. Many swingers don't wear underwear. It's a personal choice, but if you do, boxers or boxer briefs are good. Tighty whities won't get it. Neither will Speedo-type skivvies.

Women, on the other hand, are usually a lot more stylish than men. However, you might want to know that dressing for a club or a date is slightly different.

For a date, a casual but sexy outfit is fine. You can get a little sexy but I wouldn't go overboard because you have no clue as to how the other woman is going to dress. A nice, tight top that shows just a little cleavage is always good. You can pair this with a simple skirt or a pair of nice black slacks.

Now for parties and clubs, less is *always* more. A sexy little skirt or tight pants is good and the skimpier the better. (No underwear is usually a crowd pleaser.) High heels will get you a lot of looks but be warned, if you are not used to wearing them, you may end up taking them off because your feet may start aching.

As far as underwear goes, G-strings, thongs or bikinis are the norm. You don't want to wear a pair of granny panties. A nice bra with a little push-up power is good as well. And if you have a nice bra on, everyone will want to see it. You've been warned.

Wear things that accentuate your body and bring out the best in you. If you don't have the body to wear tight clothing, don't do it because these clothes will not accentuate you in the way you want to be perceived.

You want to make a good first impression. People do judge on appearances, right or wrong, they do. You want them to know *you*. You don't want them to overlook you because you look like a relic from the eighties. Looking your best will give you added confidence.

Shaving.

This goes for both women *and* men. If you want to hook up, you want to make sure you are properly groomed and that means shaving and/or trimming your pubic hair.

This is one of the biggest complaints amongst swingers. A guy once said to me, "I don't want a mouthful of hair when I'm down there."

Yeah, I was kind of taken aback myself by that comment, but he's right.

Trim and shave. Trim and shave. Use shaving gel. Start *before* you have a date or go to a club so you won't be razor burned. You should shave every day or every other day to keep it under control. It you wait too long and shave right before you go out, you are going to have razor burn. Be warned that it itches like hell.

One more thing. Men should *always, always, always* shave their faces. Women do not like to be rubbed raw by a five o'clock shadow.

Enough said.

Check yourself *before* you go out.

Before you go out, do a check on yourself to make sure your appearance is as good as it can be. You don't want to make a bad first impression because you didn't take time to brush your teeth.

I have seen people in the Lifestyle who look and smell like they didn't bother to bathe before they went out. You will probably come across them yourself. Just make sure *you're* not the one people avoid because of body odor. And they will avoid you if you're not clean.

Men, please do not use too much cologne. It is almost as big a turn-off as body odor. It can give other people headaches as well. Just a touch of cologne or aftershave is all you need. Also, if you have any facial hair, be sure to trim it up. Do this with nasal and ear hairs as well.

Women usually pay more attention to their appearance than men. However, they can overdose on perfume. Just a little is all you need.

Keep in mind pheromones are as a big a turn on as a nice scent. People want to smell *you*. Pheromones get lost if they're covered up. Your natural body scent (but not body odor) is a huge turn on for others.

Before your date, be sure to:
- Shower.
- Shave or trim facial hair.

- Shave and trim pubic hair.
- Floss and brush your teeth and use mouthwash. Don't forget to gargle.
- Check for any stray hairs in nose or ears.
- Iron clothes.
- Shine shoes.
- Trim and file nails, fingers *and* toes. (There is nothing more annoying than getting busy with someone and suddenly being gouged by their long and sharp toenails.)
- If you're a smoker, keep a pack of spearmint gum in your pocket or purse and pop it in before you meet others. But be sure to take it out *after* you meet them as you don't want to be smacking gum like Flo from *Alice* while you're trying to make conversation.
- Have your partner check your teeth for any lipstick or anything else that might be on them.

If you look your best, others will see you at your best. They will see *you* and chances are they will like what they see. And that's the impression you want. Don't sabotage yourself before you even get to the date by not taking time to look your best. *Take your time to do this.* It shows other people that you care about yourself. And that will make them want to care about fucking you.

Testing the water.

You might be reading this book and really don't have a desire to date or go to clubs. You might just want to hook up with a couple you already know. But you don't know how to break the ice. You don't even know if they're interested in swinging at all. But this is the couple you've got your heart set on.

So, how do you approach someone you already know? Test the water.

Because you already know them, you've probably invited them over to your house a few times. When you're ready to test the water, invite them again. But this time, make it a point to mention something that might give you an indication of where they stand on the issue.

You don't have to be blunt. If they're thinking the same thing you are, they're going to take the hint. And if they're not, they're going to ignore your comment.

My suggestion would be to mention and/or watch a porno. Hinting about things like swinging is always good. Hot tubs (with a glass of wine) are *always* good. You might be surprised if they say, "We've wanted to try this for years."

If they freak out and say, "Why, we'd never do anything like that!" pretend it was joke. Move on and forget it.

However, be careful. If you're too obvious about what you're talking about and they aren't hip to it, you might put your friendship at risk. Before you do anything, ask yourself if it's really worth it. Maybe it's just better to let it be a fantasy.

Related experience:
This was told to me via email.

"We knew this couple for a while and were attracted to them. But we didn't want to do anything that might make them think we were weirdoes or something and hadn't planned on ever doing anything, to be quite honest.

Well, one weekend, we took a trip together to the mountains and rented a room with a Jacuzzi. One thing lead to another and the next thing I know, we're all in the Jacuzzi naked. My husband started kissing me and the other couple started kissing as well. We didn't do a full swap, just some kissing and touching, but it was really nice."

So, just go cautiously and test the waters *before* you try anything. It's not worth losing good friends over. Okay? Okay.

Inexperience and poor choices in swing partners.

Don't be afraid to learn as you go. This is a whole new ballgame. Don't be afraid to make mistakes. The best of us make mistakes all the time. If you meet a couple and they don't work out, move on to the next one. Do not let inexperience and poor choices hinder you from giving it another try.

Another thing, if anyone ever threatens violence, walk away from it. It's not worth it.

Related experience:
As seen in a club…

I was once at a really nice club. The night was going well and everyone seemed to be having a good time. It was single guy night so the place was packed with all kinds of single dudes.

Later in the evening, I heard a commotion near the bar area. I looked over to see two guys fighting over a girl. One of the guys was her partner and the other a single guy. The single guy threw the first punch, which the partner dodged. Before it could escalate, they were escorted out of the club.

As she left, "I'm not ever doing this shit again!"

I later found out what had happened. The girl had been talking with the single guy and had mentioned wanting a threesome. She didn't say she wanted it with *him*, she just said she wanted it. He got it into his head that it was going to happen and when the couple informed him it wasn't, he got very angry.

In my opinion, she was very foolish to let this one bad experience keep her from having fun. In the first place, it wasn't her fault. Secondly, she should have known before going in that sometimes shit happens. It just does. That's life.

Don't let others rain on your parade. There are plenty of people out there who would like nothing better than to make you feel bad for your lifestyle choice. Don't let them make you feel bad. Say a silent, "Fuck off" and do as you please.

Girl/Girl

My husband says one of the best things about swinging for him is seeing me with other women. Typical male, but I completely understand. He also says if that's all we ever did, he'd be completely content with that. (Yeah, right.)

Bi-sexuality and the other term, bi-curious, is a big part of swinging. These are terms used for women who want to experience the feel of another woman, to have sex with her. I just like to call it "Playing with the girls".

If you are a woman reading this, you should realize that this issue will come up at one point or another. For some, it's icing on the cake. *Yeah! I get to have sex with girls, too!* For others, it's not something they want to dabble in. *You mean I can't play with him if I don't play with her?* Anyone would be intimidated by this—I know I certainly was—but, c'mon, you know you're curious as to what it's all about.

And what is it all about? For me, it's just another part of being a sexual being. I personally think a woman's sexuality is more fluid than a male's. And, by that I mean, it's just easier for women to like other women sexually. Also, in regards to the Lifestyle, bi-sexuality in a woman is certainly more encouraged than it is in males. Men love to see their women kissing and feeling another woman. They love to see them give another woman oral sex or receive it in turn. (And let's don't even get started on the touching of breasts…) It's a *huge* turn on for men. Any man who says it's not is lying. Or extraordinarily repressed.

(I once met a guy at a club who told me he really didn't care for "that kind of thing" and he "didn't see the big deal". Later on, his wife was dirty dancing with another woman—topless—and he could not take his eyes off them. So much for not being into "that kind of thing".)

And, if you're a woman, it's an opportunity to see why men love women so much. After my first experience with another woman, I finally understood. Other women are soft and delicious and great to play with. I told my husband, "I see why you love women! We're so soft and nice!" He couldn't have agreed more. After you do it, it just seems so natural. And you'll want to do it again.

Again, the choice is yours.

Many couples get into swinging so the female can explore this part of her sexuality. Some are only interested in other females for threesomes or just for girl/girl play. I have been asked by many couples just to have sex with the woman as that's all they're into. (Usually the male wants to watch.) This is not unusual. But for many women out there, it's a hindrance. Some women are not interested in playing with other girls and miss out on many swinging chances because they are not bi-sexual or even bi-curious.

Again, again, the choice is entirely up to you. Some women don't like it. Some do. Whatever choice you make is fine. If you're invited to join in on some girl/girl play and don't want to partake, be polite and decline. Others will understand and find someone else to play with.

My personal opinion is that a woman should try it at least once. *This is only my opinion, though.* She won't know what she's missing out on if she doesn't. However, if this isn't your cup of tea, don't do it. If the issue comes up and you don't want to do it, then don't do it. It's really no big deal.

Question to ask yourself.

If you're still reading this book, chances are you want to try swinging. The question to ask yourself here is: *Do you have the guts?*

Remember to be completely honest.

The bi-sexual man.

If you're a male and want to explore sex with other men, be warned that this is only a tiny part of the Lifestyle. In fact, it's somewhat discouraged. In fact, I have never heard of another man having sex with another man at a swing party or club. On this front, there is just not much I can discuss because I have not been a witness to this part of swinging.

Related experience:

This is Jennifer's story.

"We had this great threesome with a single guy, who I thought was completely straight. Well, we invited him back a few times and each time he'd try to get closer and closer to my husband. He wanted to get closer to me as well. I didn't really think anything about it. Well, come to find out, this guy had a crush on my husband as well as a crush on me! He wanted to move in with us. He wanted to be my boyfriend and my husband's...uh, boyfriend. Sounds weird, but it's completely true.

Needless to say, it didn't work out. My husband is as straight as an arrow. He declined and the guy went on his way. I felt bad for him but we're a couple first and foremost. There's not room in our relationship for another person."

That about sums it up.

Threesomes.

Which one do you prefer? Male/female/male (MFM) or female/male/female (FMF)? The choice is yours but you might want to try both. I know for me, having a threesome is a total mind-blowing experience. When you're doing a threesome, it's like having hands and lips stimulating you at all times. And you can be penetrated while kissing (or sucking) someone else. There is so much enjoyment for all involved.

So what if all you and your partner want is a threesome? There are many different ways to go about this, including attending swinging events.

It should be noted, that for a couple, hooking up with another male is going to be easier than hooking up with another female. It simply means men are more willing to do threesomes than women. And, no, it doesn't mean either male is gay if he wants this.

One male at a party explained it to me, "I loved watching her getting fucked while she was sucking my cock. I loved seeing her do it. It made me realize what a sexual being she is and it made me love and respect her even more."

Cool.

Hooking up with a male at a party or club should be easy-peasy. Just approach your choice for the evening and ask him about it. He'll either say yes or he'll say no. Most men will jump at this chance. You can also put an ad out explaining you are looking for single men for threesome action.

As far as finding an attractive female to make your dreams come true, this is going to be harder. Though it is far from being impossible, it is going to be trickier than finding a male. Get ready to begin the search. Many couples post on their ads "Single females wanted". Others go to parties and/or clubs looking to hook up.

So if you want a female/male/female threesome, my advice to you is to first advertise on a swinger site. See what kind of response you get. If you don't get what you're looking for, maybe go to a swing party or a club. The women there are usually very approachable and I believe this is your best bet.

I was very lucky with my first threesome. A couple we swung with wanted a threesome and we agreed to swap just in this capacity, the men taking turns getting a threesome with the girls. It was hot and by the end of the night, we were exhausted. (But we made the guys buy us breakfast, so that made up for it.)

But if this isn't your scene, you are going to have a harder time getting it done. I won't go as far as saying hiring an escort for the night, but if you find yourself in Nevada...then that's your business.

I could recommend that you invite a close girlfriend to join you. She should be as sexually liberated as you, though. Even then, it may be difficult to deal with the person afterwards. She might feel guilty and break off the friendship. It might be better to approach someone who's just an acquaintance. And it might be wise to have the female approach her and feel her out. You should be able to tell if she's into it.

You might also go to a regular club to find someone. I knew one couple who did this all the time. I asked how they did it: "We go to a club, hang out and pick out a nice looking girl. My girlfriend approaches her and asks if we can buy her a drink. At this point, she knows what's up and she either comes over or she declines. If she declines, we find someone else. If she accepts, we drink a little, the girls dance and we invite her back to our hotel room. (We never take them to our house.) And we have some great sex. Lots of times, they ask for our number so we can get together again, but other times, we never see them again. It's totally up to her."

Whichever route you decide to take, be assured that you will eventually get what you want. If you get turned down, try, try again and don't be discouraged.

Single men. Yes or no?

Single men are guys who are looking to get into the Lifestyle as a swinger in order to partake in all the crazy sex. They usually don't have girlfriends or wives and if they do, the wives or girlfriends don't participate in the Lifestyle with them. Single men vary in age, race and size.

I think it's a good idea but usually it never turns out right because single men can be a bit weird. They may develop a crush on the female or they may put down your lifestyle choice or they may just be assholes. The ones I have come in contact with are overbearing and they think that just because you're there, you'll want to fuck them.

Some are nice and affable. Some aren't. And, unfortunately, most can be very, very pushy and don't like to take "no" for an answer. This is why many swinging couples do not like single men. In fact, many clubs and parties have a ban on single guys because they can be overbearing and really bring everyone down.

Personal experience:
One of the first swing clubs I went to was full of single men. My partner had left for a moment to go get some drinks and I sat on a couch in the TV room and watched the porno. He wasn't gone two minutes before I had two single guys on either side of me. Both tried to converse with me and it even seemed as if they were competing or my attention. I should have been flattered, but to be honest, it made me uneasy.

At first, I was nice as this is my nature. One of the guys must have realized he was wasting his time (I don't do moustaches) and left. Well, that only spurred this other guy on. It was like he had won a prize or something. I finally set him straight and told him I wasn't interested but he would not let up. He kept at me. He decided he wanted me and he'd paid *all* this money to get in the club. I guess he figured he wanted to get something out of it, *at my expense.*

I finally decided to turn him down again and move away from him. I did. He followed me all around the club, even after my partner rejoined me. He wouldn't let up and kept badgering me, telling me how he could "rock my world" and all kinds of stupid stuff. Finally, I couldn't take it anymore and said, "I do not want to have sex with you. Please leave me alone." And he replied, "Why did you come here if you didn't want to have sex?"

What he couldn't get through his head was that I did want to have sex. Just not with him.

Okay, the point is, you can't let these guys have any leverage. Remember, you are in control. You have the power to say yes or no. It is your decision and yours alone. You do not have to make excuses to these people.

A good rule of thumb: After you've met them and decided you're not going to do anything with them, excuse yourself and find someone else to talk to. Single men can be very convincing and they won't mind pulling out all the stops to get you to do what they want. As I've said, they've paid a lot of money to be there and they want something out of it, regardless of whether or not you do.

They have the *club* mentality. This means these guys will follow women around and badger them until they're worn down enough to have sex with them. They act like they're at a night club.

DON'T BE AFRAID TO SAY NO! Furthermore, don't be afraid to look like a bitch. So what if you piss some guy off? Did you really want to have sex with him? If not, move on. Don't worry. If he can't handle rejection, he shouldn't have come in the first place.

Single guys are sometimes not just looking for sex, but for a relationship. They can be overbearing and they do not care to make a fool out of themselves if they think it will get them laid.

Related experience:

As told to me at a swing party.

"The last swing party we attended was really crowded and we had to park at the far end of the drive and walk up a steep hill to get to it. A lot of older swingers were there so we knew we pretty much weren't going to hook up. We decided to stay and just have a good time, you know?

Well, all night this guy, who had to be about twenty years older than me, stuck by my side. I even later found out that he had asked my husband if he could have sex with me and my husband had told him I made those decisions for myself and he had to ask me himself. My husband didn't want to hurt his feelings, I guess. And he figured the guy would get the hint. He didn't. He asked me to have sex with him and I declined. Maybe I was too nice to him because he hovered around me all night. He wasn't weird or mean or anything, just annoying.

We decided to leave around midnight. We found the hosts and told them thank-you and all that. Well, the guy kind of hung around as we were saying goodbye to all the people we'd met. And as soon as we left, he got in step with us and walked us to our car. Only later did we realize that he had done that so it would look like he was leaving with us! Like we were all three going somewhere to have sex! It's funny when you get right down to it. How desperate can you be? Poor guy."

Yeah, poor guy. It's hard not to feel sorry for some of them, but don't let your empathy keep you from hooking up with someone who really turns you on.

On the other hand, what if you're a single man looking to get into this? Don't be discouraged. You can do it, but you are going to have to be one helluva guy. A guy everyone wants around. If you're good looking, funny and are not looking for a relationship, i.e. not looking to steal someone's woman, this is a good place for you to go and have fun. But be warned, everyone is already cautious of you because others before you have fucked it up. You could be the one to turn this whole attitude towards single men around.

You have to be cool. You have to dress and smell nice. You have to willing to hang back and let people come to you. Make eye contact, smile and maybe even say hello. But do not hover, do not push and do not make an annoyance of yourself. And if someone says no, listen to them and move away.

Related experience:

This comes from a single guy.

I was at this party and there were about ten couples there. I kept getting the cold shoulder because, I guess, I was the only single guy.

It's not that anyone was rude; it was just as if everyone had their guard up around me. Later on, everyone went upstairs (I'm assuming to have group sex) and left me by myself in the living room. I just hung around hoping that something would happen for me. The host came down a little later, stopped in the door and gave me a, *You're still here?!* look. I felt like one hundred percent crap.

I got up and left. I had only gone to the party for sex. I wasn't looking for a relationship and they had invited me! They didn't have to treat me like I had the plague or something.

Well, I felt really bad. Not only had I wasted an evening but I had also wasted a lot of money to get there and nothing happened. I should have known better."

Unfortunately, this is the kind of stuff that happens to a lot of single guys. You have to realize that, as a single guy, people will have their guard up around you. Most likely, it's because something has happened to this couple involving a single guy. It's usually not nice and probably made the couple feel like shit. No one likes a bad swing experience, especially involving single men.

Therefore, all single men should be civil and wait to be approached or at least wait until someone shows some interest before they attempt to do anything. And if no one shows interest, *take the hint and leave.* Don't sit around and wait for "something to happen". It's probably not going to. Be smart enough to know when to call it a night.

As for clubs, do not hound the women that are there. *Do not* put them down for their lifestyle choice because they turned you down and *do not* judge them for it. You're there too, after all. Doesn't that make *you* a swinger as well? You have to be as open-minded, if not more so, than the couple swingers in there.

Do not ever try to talk women into having sex with you. If they want you, they will let you know. Believe me, they will let you know. Otherwise, keep your distance. Just go to have fun and if something happens, that's icing on the cake. And if it doesn't, so what? You could spend a lot of money in a "normal" club and nothing could happen there either. You're not there to "get your money's worth". You're there because the hosts and/or owners allow you to be there. And do you really want to be perceived as a creep? Because if you hound women and try to talk them into doing something they obviously don't want to do with you, you will be labeled a creep and no one will want anything to do with you after that.

This may sound a little harsh but wouldn't you rather hear it here first before you go and make an ass out of yourself in public? I know I would.

Personally, I would love for more single men to join in on the Lifestyle. Men who want to party and only party, that is. It adds to the variety. It's just most of the ones I've met have not been what I'm looking for. Many women in the Lifestyle might agree.

So, I am certainly not discouraging single men from pursuing this kind of lifestyle. I'm only saying if you do, you need to have your head out of your ass and adopt a laid back attitude.

Single women.

A lot of single women come to clubs and parties just to check it out. Some go because they are exhibitionists and want to show off. Most of these women are cute and likeable. I don't think I've ever met one rude single woman. Keep in mind, they are *not* there to "get your man". They are usually just there to join in on the action with other women or during group sex.

Single women are, without fail, invited to events because they add to the excitement. They usually get in for free and are usually always welcome.

Personal experience:
A few years ago, I was at a party where single women were invited. There was this cute Asian girl who had shed her clothes as soon as she walked into the room. She had recently had a boob job and wanted everyone to feel. I felt her boobs and we had a silly conversation, then most of the women took off their tops and proceeded to dance in the middle of the room as the guys watched. We felt each other up and had a great time. She later used a butterfly vibrator on me. *Nice* memory.

On the other hand...

Related experience:

Overheard at a party.

A couple decided to have a threesome with a girl they'd just recently met. They had a great time and the girl became a weekend guest. However, it soon became evident that she didn't just want sex, she wanted a relationship. She asked the couple if she could move in with them. They conceded because they thought she was a really nice girl and she needed help. They were unaware of her feelings. A few months later, the female of the couple finds out that this girl is tearing her home life apart. She decided that she wanted this woman's life and was even trying to get the husband to leave his wife. The couple, in the end, sorted their problems with the girl out and after much trouble, got her out of their house, but not without some emotional damage.

My advice is this: *Never, and I repeat never, invite another person into your relationship.* No matter how nice they are. No matter how "in need" they seem, keep it separate.

You can be friends but beyond that, it can get weird and/or complicated.

Cliques.

No, you haven't been transported back to high school, nor are you attending your class reunion. It's sad but true, cliques are a big part of the Lifestyle.

It's like this. You go to a club or a party and find that you don't know anyone there. And all these people have separated themselves from everyone else. And they always seem to be having the best damn time, too. Nobody's talking to you or paying you any attention at all. You suddenly feel like that sixteen year old kid at the pep rally who didn't "fit in" with the "in" crowd.

Note: Just because they're young and cool doesn't necessarily they're going to be great swinging partners.

If you find yourself in a roomful of cliques, you can do one or two things. You can leave or you can take your chances and approach them and try to start a conversation. Be warned that some people can be just as rude as they were in high school. They have their group and usually don't want to let anyone else in. These cliques rarely open their doors to new people. If you want to join in on a clique, keep in mind that, at first, people have to get to know you. You might have to be introduced and then invited in. A lot of the time, it's just not worth the trouble. My advice? Go talk to other people who aren't cliqued up.

It has always bothered me that cliques are a part of swinging because it so goes against what swinging is all about: Meeting new people and enjoying new experiences with them.

Personal experience:

We once attended a swing party that started out at a bar, and then would go to a hotel close by. When we first arrived, there was nobody else in the bar except for us. We just figured we were early and that everybody would start getting there soon. They didn't.

It was beginning to get late and we wondered if the event had been canceled. About thirty minutes later, a few couples showed up.

We introduced ourselves but found the other people a little off-putting. Soon, about four other couples were there and they pretty much roped themselves off at another table, only occasionally glancing our way. At first, we couldn't believe this was happening. It just didn't seem right. We gave it a little time, trying not to cringe in embarrassment and hoped something would change. We got a few drinks at the bar, stopped at their table and tried to make conversation. But they really didn't respond to anything we were saying. They gave us tight smiles and, it appeared, didn't really want anyone to join in on their group.

What could we do? It was obvious we had found ourselves in clique hell. We did the smart thing and left, taking time to explore the new town we were in and had a wonderful time. By ourselves.

Just put yourself out there because you never know what will happen. And if you're turned down, or find yourself in clique hell, please don't let this deter you from trying again. Remember, they don't know you and may have their own reasons for being cliquish. You *have* to be wary to a certain extent of people you don't know. Don't judge. Just move on and enjoy the rest of your night. Always rely on your instincts. If the people seem unapproachable, they usually are.

Signs you're being taken advantage of.

It's inevitable. The more you put yourself out there, the more likely you are going to get burned at some time or another. It happens. There are people out there who will take advantage of you. When I first started swinging, I didn't even consider this because I had the idea that most people who swung were the coolest people on earth. Many are. Some aren't.

Let me reiterate: *There are people out there who will take advantage of you.* There may be extenuating circumstances, there may not be. There are good people out there who simply don't have the money to swing. It could not be monetary at all. It could be that they are just insensitive. Ask yourself, *Are they worth the effort?*

Signs you are being taken advantage of:
- You always pick up the tab for dinner.
- You invite them to your house and cook. They never bring anything with them.
- They ask for personal favors.
- You are always emailing first and last.
- Many times, your emails are not responded to.
- They never reciprocate on any level.

Personal experience:
A few years after we started swinging, we were contacted by email by this couple who seemed great. We had a soft swing

the first night, then the next time, we did a full swap. It was a nice time and we enjoyed their company so much, we began to occasionally invite them to our house and cook for them. We did this a lot but began to notice that they never invited *us* to their house.

They always wanted to spend the night and being the good hosts we are we'd get up early and cook breakfast. They'd rise, take long showers, then come downstairs for breakfast, and then would lounge around afterwards, talking and watching TV. At first, this was okay because we really liked them. After a while, it began to get old and we eventually stopped seeing them because we felt we were being taken advantage of.

Related experience:

Shortly after I met him, Tony told me this story.

"We met this really nice couple through an internet ad and met them at a bar one night. After that, we started seeing them on a regular basis. They were okay lovers, nothing to brag about but they were nice and sometimes that's enough, you know?

The thing I didn't like was that when our date or whatever would be over, they'd say, 'Let's do it again. How about next week?' Well, they would never email, so I'd have to do it and it would take them days to get back to us. And they would usually email back on the day we'd given up on them and decided to do something else. We were always the ones contacting them. I wanted to stop seeing them after a while, but my wife insisted we give it a try because she said, 'Good friends are really hard to find.' I conceded. Well, the next time they told us to give them a call, I decided I wasn't going to do it to see if they would call us. Guess what? They never did.

We wasted a lot of time on them. But you live and learn. I guess they weren't *that* nice."

Good words. Live and learn.

Something else to consider is that another couple might not be as interested in you as you are in them. *Don't take it personally.* This does happen and it happens to the best of us. We all want to do everything in our power to make them like us. You can get taken advantage of if you have this mentality. We overcompensate so they'll like us more and want to be our friends. I've done it myself. But the more you do, the more they will expect. This is natural. However, other people shouldn't expect you to. And if they don't offer to reciprocate every once in a while, they're losers and not worth dealing with. They should like you for who you are, *not* for what you do for them.

Also, you can't expect complete honesty from other people, especially in swinging, but you should expect it from your partner who should expect it in turn.

If you are only into this to get friends, you have picked the wrong thing to go into. Friendship can come later, but at first, you need to worry about getting laid, plain and simple. Always remember, you don't *have* to be friends. This is the mistake I made at first, thinking I had to be friends first and lovers later. It's a common mistake that can cause you a lot of pain. Not to mention a lot of time. Friends first usually means you're not going to get laid and if you do, things are going to get weird. It will become too personal.

Don't ever forget that swinging is about sex, first and foremost. Realize this is a very complex dynamic. People can and will get weird. It could be due to a number of things. They could be having trouble themselves with the Lifestyle. They could be having troubles you would never imagine yourself having.

Personal experience:

Not too long ago, we swung with a couple and became good friends with them. Or so we thought. We were a few months into the friendship when it started getting weird. I noticed that they would ask to "borrow" things all the time, which was fine, but kinda odd at the same time. Odder still, they would never return the borrowed items. They would also cancel our dates at the last minute. They wouldn't return emails. This would have been fine if we never heard from them again or they had come right out and told us they didn't want to pursue the friendship anymore.

But they'd send emails out of the blue, expecting us to drop everything and see them. Being the nice people—or fools—we were, we'd always do it. Towards the end, I was fed up with being a nice person and when they wanted to have lunch one Saturday on the premise of returning some videos, we went. I was polite but not overly friendly. At the end of lunch, the female leaned over and asked for our address so she could mail the videos to us that they'd forgotten to bring. This told us they were no long interested in being our friends, which was more than fine with us. To top it off, the next day, we received a nasty email from them saying, among other things, that I was rude, we were too needy and they just didn't have the time to see us every weekend. They said some other things I don't care to rehash.

Goodbye to you, too.

Things can get sticky, especially when you throw sex into the mix. We simply got too close. Perhaps, we wanted to be friends with these people more than swing partners.

Swinging can bring out the worse in people. I've witnessed this over and over. They may be nice people but, as I've said, when you throw sex in there, it can get nasty.

Related experience:
A close swinging friend of mine had a similar experience.

"Well, we met this couple, on the internet, of course, and they seemed cool so we set up a date with them. Though the guy was not really my type, I thought, *Why not go ahead and give it a try?* So we did a full swap and the guy couldn't get hard, which was fine with me. I mean, it's really no big deal and we can try again later. I was more into her than I was him anyway.

Well, this continued to happen for a while and my husband and I talked it out and decided we wouldn't have sex with them anymore. I mean, the guy couldn't get hard, so I wasn't having sex anyway. So we told them we were taking a break. Well, they insisted (or persuaded) us to see them as "friends".

Now every time we saw them, it would always end up with sex. I mean my husband and her having sex. I didn't get to have sex cause the guy couldn't get hard. I began to get frustrated. I mean, I don't even know how it happened. But every time, we'd all end up naked and my husband and her would have sex and I would feel left out. Even after we told them we didn't want to it would happen. Maybe we drank too much and thought, *Hell, he might be able to do it this time.*

He never was able to, though.

One night she made me really mad. After a 'session', we were all sitting around feeling bad because the guy couldn't get hard. My husband felt bad about it and said, 'We can try again later.' And the woman snapped, 'No, we can't! We're done for the night!'

We were taken aback. In fact, I was pretty pissed off. No one talks to my man like that. (Except for me, of course. Just kidding!) I realized then that she was a fake. Anyone who is that super sweet to your face is usually a fake. No one is that nice! She showed her true colors that night.

We never saw them again after that.

After I gained some perspective, I realized what they were doing. They were using us to work out their 'problems' with swinging. They wanted to be swingers but had some sort of roadblock in their way. It might have been jealousy or insecurity, I don't know what it was, but I do know it was unfair of them to put us through that. They used us to workshop their problems. That's why they insisted on seeing us and always having sex. Even after we told them we didn't want to have sex anymore. I think we just felt sorry for them and went through with it.

I guess the moral of the story is, you should do what you want to do, otherwise you end up feeling used, like we did. To begin with, I wasn't that sexually attracted to the guy and just went along with it. And though the couple was nice on the surface, there were just other places I wanted to be. Sorry, but that's the way I feel. I mean, why waste all that time? It just doesn't make sense to me to do stuff like that anymore. I mean, I want everyone to have a good time but I want to have a good time, too. I want something out of it as much as the next person."

It should be noted that some swingers are friends with each other. It really depends on who you click with. I would stress caution, though, when you first meet someone. Really feel them out. (Maybe after you've felt them up.)

Ask yourself this: Is the sex good? Do you enjoy spending time with this couple? And, most importantly, what are you getting out of it? If you're having a good time, keep that friendship, it could last years. We're friends with many swingers whom we've never swung with as well as with ones we have. It really, really depends on the people. It's just like any other sort of relationship in that regard.

Keep in mind, most people are just into this lifestyle for the sex and they already have their "straight" friends. Lots of people like to keep it separate. If this is your preference, make no excuses for it. Be polite if you don't want to see the other couple as much as they want to see you. Use your instincts. If you hit it off, fine, but it is not necessary for a successful swinging experience.

Always remember, some people can handle swinging and some people can't. And *never* take it personally.

How often should I swing?

There is certain etiquette to swinging. Many things that apply to "normal" situations don't necessarily apply to swinging. An important thing to keep in mind is frequency. How often should you swing? This depends on you. There is no hard and fast rule to it.

You can do it as often as you and your partner like. As I've said earlier, it's all about your choices. You can do it every week or every month or every other month or once a year. It's entirely up to you.

On the other side of this, you might have met a couple you really click with and would like to see them as much as possible. It's easy to get overly involved with another couple and allow yourself to become exclusive with them. In my opinion, this is not a good idea. Things can and will get weird.

So, how often should you swing with the same couple? A good rule of thumb is no more than once a month. This allows you distance and time to breathe and organize your thoughts. If you see them every single weekend, you might become too familiar and it may seem like there's a little more than just sex involved. Someone might get jealous. If you do it more than once a month, it's *almost* like you're in a relationship with them. This is bad news. Bad, bad news.

Personal experience:

Right after we started swinging, we met this really nice couple. (Keep in mind that they're *always* nice to begin with.) Everything was going so good that we saw each other every weekend. *Yes, every weekend.* We didn't have enough experience to know when to take a break. Or to know that we *should* have taken a break.

They were great. We had long, intelligent talks and laughed and flirted a lot. We had same room sex and did full swaps. It was fun.

This went on for a couple of months and then everything went to hell. The other female began to act weird and I'd notice she would never let her husband have a minute alone with me.

Which was fine, but strange. (I wasn't looking to marry the guy. I just wanted to fuck him. Besides, she was fucking *my* husband.) She got very territorial. On the last night we were going to see them, we'd pretty much decided that this would be it because we'd noticed the change in their behavior.

The night began normally enough, and then dissolved into chaos.

We were playing strip poker and I got to take my top off first. She gave me an odd look and said, "Oh, she always wants to take her top off. I think she cheated."

I just looked at her. What was she getting at?

She stared back and snapped, "Isn't that right? You like to show off in front of my husband, don't you?"

Well, I kind of thought that was the point. Nonetheless, her comment unnerved me.

To make a long story short, the female accused me of being in love with her husband and all this other stuff. I accused her of being jealous. Fortunately (or unfortunately for the guys) before a full blown catfight could ensue, we left.

We got too close. Swinging can be highly emotional in the first place and things can get weird if you get too close. Whenever you throw sex into the mix of things, it changes the nature of your relationship, whether you're single, married or swinging. But in swinging, my personal opinion is that if you get too close to another couple, it can most likely make things get weird.

This is because everyone—including yourself—may not be quite as open and secure as they might think. You need to even it

out. It's like eating rich food. A little bit is great, but if you eat too much too fast, you might just find yourself getting sick.

Remember, this is about you and your partner. Let other couples deal with their own problems on their own time. Everyone should be there to have a good time, first and foremost. And if they're acting weird, chances are, they're not having a good time and aren't really into it.

My advice is to not get too personal too soon. Ease into it. Never forget that it's just about sex. It is about you and your lover expanding boundaries and simply getting off. One nice lady I met at a party put it like this, "I love my husband very much, but why would I want another one? This is just about me having fun, him having fun and us leaving together. I like to think of it as using another person to help me get off. Their body, their hands are nice, but they could never replace my husband."

She's right. In an odd way, you are using another person's body to get off. You already have a relationship so why would you want another one?

Related experience:

Allison told me this story at a club.

"Yeah, when we first started swinging, we got too close to a couple. When we first started seeing them, we all agreed to go to swing clubs together. Because all of us were so new, we thought going to clubs together would take the edge off and we could help each other out by being there for one another.

Well, a month or so later, I casually mentioned a club I'd found on the internet. The husband gave me a weird look, so I didn't pursue it and we kept seeing them, though any time my husband or I would mention going to a club or party, they would act like they really weren't interested. Which would be fine, but they had agreed, at first, to do this. One time, I mentioned that we were going to meet another couple, just to see what they'd do and they freaked out, saying that they wouldn't have slept with us if they had known we were bedpost notchers. They also said they were terrified of getting diseases and couldn't understand why we would want to do such a thing.

They basically wanted us to themselves, which is a very creepy feeling, I can assure you. In fact, I didn't know this was an exclusive relationship. We broke it off and went to a swing club by ourselves and had a great time without them."

Remember, the point of swinging is to have a variety of experiences. *Not just one with one couple.* If you feel things are getting a little sticky, tell them you're taking a break and take one. It is always important to give yourself, and others, room to breathe.

Swing rule #2.

You must go into swinging for the right reasons. And those reasons include wanting to get closer to your lover and to get in touch with who you really are and the sexual being inside yourself.

Signs that things are going bad:

- You and your partner are arguing more.
- You've stopped having sex with each other.
- You never laugh or have fun as a couple.
- Someone is holding a grudge, either you or your partner.
- You're not communicating.
- Your life is tensed and strained.
- You can't take a joke.
- The thought of swinging is confusing you.
- You find yourself disassociating yourself from swinging, i.e., you were "never there". You were "talked" into it. You didn't "want to do it in the first place".
- You condemn the swinging lifestyle for no real reason.
- You see other swingers as being more than what they are: More evil, more malicious, more devious, and more lustful.
- You don't trust your partner.

If swinging is making you or your partner feel any of these things, you might consider getting out. It is not worth your relationship. Your relationship is much, much more important than swinging.

If you talk to your partner and he/she is not responding, take a breath, don't get upset and tell them exactly how you feel. If they love and care for you, they will listen to you.

If they want to continue when you don't, you need to make them understand your reasons. You should realize that *whatever reasons you have are fine.* If you can't make them understand and they insist you continue when you don't want to, refuse. This is as much a personal decision as it is a couple decision and you should not be forced into something you don't want to do.

Remember, this is a very complicated dynamic. It brings out a lot of emotion and how you deal with that emotion is paramount to how you deal with swinging.

If you simply don't like it, give yourself permission to stop. It's not a drug and you won't need re-hab to get over it. Once you make the decision to discontinue in the Lifestyle, you can get back to your normal life.

Maybe you just like the idea of the Lifestyle without the participation. Maybe you just like hanging out with swingers. Maybe you just like to watch. Remember, there are options in the Lifestyle. However, if none of it agrees with you at all, your best option may be to get out.

Most importantly, don't drive yourself crazy with guilt. Swinging is not wrong. And what you did is not wrong, either. *Don't beat yourself up over it.* Pat yourself on the back for giving it a try and move on with your life. You can always refer to your swinging experience as, "That crazy thing I tried once." It will, more than likely, give you a good feeling.

Crying in the corner.

I overheard this at a party: "But honey, this is what we're *here* for." Shortly thereafter, the couple left. I later found out that *he* wasn't into it and *she* was. He got mad, pouted and made her leave the party.

What a crybaby.

You've had a nice night, and then something happens. Someone gets mad or jealous. This is commonly referred to as "Crying in the corner." Usually it involves a female who can't handle something she's just seen or a male who is angry at something his lover has done. I've seen couples fight. I've seen yelling matches. It's not pretty and usually brings everyone at the party down. Though this doesn't happen that often, sometimes situations will arise that take the fun out of swinging.

When this happens, I usually just turn a blind eye and hope no one gets hurt. If I find someone crying in the bathroom, I try to console them, but if they tell me to leave them alone, I leave them alone.

Usually, the situation will take care of itself. Couples who fight leave the party early or work it out amongst themselves. But what if that someone is *you*?

Uh oh.

Something has happened. Your night is ruined. You saw your lover kissing someone else and it made you...well, *angry*. Maybe someone said something rude to you. Or maybe you said something rude to someone else. And now you feel awful.

Note: *Suffering is easy. Don't play the martyr!*

Keep in mind:
- Keep a stiff upper lip.
- Don't embarrass yourself.
- Don't embarrass your partner.
- You are an adult. Act like one!

Again, with feeling, swinging is a complex dynamic. It will bring out feelings you never even thought about having. The first time I saw my partner kissing another woman, I thought I was going to throw up. But I lived through the moment and it got easier and after a while, I was cool with it. Before our first swing encounter, I was sure I was going to freak out when I saw him having sex with someone else. I felt sure I would run from the room and collapse into hysterical sobs. But I didn't. I was too busy having sex myself.

Any kind of relationship—sexual or non—takes time. It takes time to get to know new people and, more importantly, it takes times to get to know the "new" partner you have now, the one who a year or so ago might not have ever imagined themselves in this kind of lifestyle. It also takes time to get to know the *new you*.

People do change and swinging can bring that change about swiftly. One day you think you know someone and the next, they've *changed.*

Depending on whether it's a good, positive change or not varies with each individual couple. For us, it was a positive change. For a few others we know, no. We even know a couple who divorced because of swinging.

Please note that I am in no way trying to discourage you from taking advantage of the swinging Lifestyle. But you need to be aware of the risks involved. You have to be prepared to deal with that.

My advice is to live through the feelings. *They will pass.* After they pass, ask yourself, *Can I handle that again?* If it's a resounding *NO!,* you might consider thinking about taking a break from swinging until you *can* handle it. You might even consider that you may never be able to handle it. Many people can't. Everyone isn't cut out for it. It's nothing to be ashamed of.

Ask yourself why you're having a problem with it and talk to your partner about it. Maybe you just need to be reassured.

Remember, you may want to come back to this party or club, don't ruin it by being a crybaby. Take your problems outside the room and deal with them away from the party. *You should have discussed any problems you thought you might have before you went to the party.* Don't make everyone else feel bad because you can't handle it. You don't want to get yourself labeled because nobody wants to be around a crybaby. If you do something erratic, no one will invite you back. This is a fact. Everyone is there to have a good time. Period. They are not there to deal with your problems. Take your problems out of the room.

This happens to the best of us, how you deal with it is up to you.

Related experience:

This was told to me to on a date:

"We were seeing this couple pretty regularly. They were cool. One day we were out on the boat and they got in an argument and the chick put her cigarette out on the guy's dick! We were just shocked. How could she do that? And what if she got mad at one of us? We made our excuses and cut the date short and, of course, we never saw them again.

But why did she do it? Hell, I don't know! She never offered an excuse. I think she was just nuts. Jealousy is one thing, but this was entirely different."

Crazy stuff does happen but don't let it happen to you. Keep your eyes and ears open and be prepared to walk away from any situation that makes you uneasy.

When things go right.

There is no greater sense of freedom you will experience when you discover that you can handle swinging and that you *like* it. You will feel extremely good that you have gotten over your hang-ups. A sense of relief will wash over you and will accompany this feeling of elation. Relief? Yes. Relief that you had the balls to go through with it and not succumbed to jealousy or anger. And you're looking forward to doing it again.

You will be as giddy as a schoolchild.

Signs that things are going right:
- You can't stop smiling.
- You and your lover are having mind blowing sex.
- You can't wait to do it again.
- You've started an exercise regime and are sticking to it.
- The little things at work and home just don't bother you as much.
- You are seeing your lover in a whole new light. And you like it very much.
- You aren't as materialistic.
- Television shows and movies make you roll their eyes when they discuss sex.
- You're considering other sexual adventures you never thought you'd be interested in: Group sex, girl-girl, threesomes, etc…

- You want to tell the whole world about it, but know you can't tell but are glad you have such a delicious secret.
- You wonder why you didn't try it sooner.

All I can say is congratulations. You've come a long way, baby.

Swinging is the best stress relief. I know when I finally got over all my hang-ups and finally swung, I was so de-stressed that people at work asked me what I was doing to be so refreshed. I thought, *Wouldn't you like to know?*

Are you suited for the swinging?

By now you should have a pretty good idea whether or not you're suited to be a swinger. But the only real way to know for sure is to give it a try.

Note: *You can't know how you feel about it until you actually do it.*

Not suited for the Lifestyle.

One of my biggest peeves with swinging is people who insist on going into it knowing full well they are not suited. These people will cause you a lot of pain. And, yes, this happens more than you think.

And by not being suited, I mean, they know from the get-go that they are jealous, insecure people. Or maybe they don't know themselves that well and that's the problem. These people don't mind hurting other people, either. They will put up a good front, too, so you usually don't find out about them until you've been screwed.

For some reason, these people think swinging is something they *should* do. Even though they probably don't enjoy it, they continue to do it. Whatever the reason they've settled on, they are dead wrong.

Usually, they've given it a few tries and failed miserably because they couldn't handle it, which is more than fine. But they keep on trying, hurting people left and right and not caring about the pain they cause.

If you know beyond a shadow of a doubt that you are not suited for swinging but go into it anyway, you should have your ass kicked. Plain and simple. Harsh words but I hope this message gets across because it is one of the most important things to understand. You will end up hurting people because of your insecurities and if you're a very insecure person, swinging isn't a valid choice for you.

You have to a *very* strong individual to swing. You have to be a person who *likes* the thought of living on the edge, who is *willing* to take chances and live with the consequences, whatever they may be. You have to be a person willing to live in the moment and not hold on to grudges. You have to be a person who likes other people, men *and women*. You have to be a bigger person. *Being petty and small-minded is not going to cut it in swinging.*

Also, you have to have a strong bond with your partner. You have to like, if not love, the thought of your partner having sex with someone else. You have to know beyond a shadow of doubt that you love your partner and they love you.

It should be noted that most of the trouble does arise from other women. It occasionally happens to men, too. I've seen it in both.

But for the most part, there are women out there who simply don't like other women. They don't want their partners doing anything with anyone but them. They get pissed off and make everyone's life miserable because they, themselves, like swinging and think they are entitled to it. They just don't like it for their partner.

If you don't read anything else in this book, please read the following related experience. It may save you a lot of pain.

Related experience:
Becky is a close friend of mine.

"God, it was awful. It went on for months and months. I almost lost my marriage over it. It didn't stop me from swinging because I *am* suited, but it made me doubt myself and, more importantly, it made me doubt my husband, whom I've never doubted before in my life.

This couple—I don't even know how to describe them—but this couple had baggage. Way more than they should have had. We didn't know this going in, but by the end, we wished we'd never met them and I've never said that about anyone else before in my life.

Of course, it started out fine. A full swap on the second date. Then another full swap on the next. Everything seemed fine on the surface, but there was this underlying current I can't describe. An uneasiness. It was like they acted like they were glad to have us, but, at the same time, they didn't really want us around. It was unnerving. Like, we spent the night with them one night and the next morning at breakfast, the guy had a hangover and I said, 'You'll feel better later,' thinking that would make him feel better. And he snapped at me, 'I *know* I'll feel better later, but right now I feel awful!' Like I was a dumbass for pointing that out.

He was pissed, that's all. I know now he was pissed at his wife and he'd taken it out on me.

They were very, very secretive about their past swing experiences, too, though they claimed to be very experienced. I can only hope they didn't have the opportunity to drive the other couples they were with as crazy like they drove us. I hope we're the only ones who went through this with them. I'd hate to think of other couples dealing with what we dealt with. It was that bad.

It was really hard to figure them out because they never showed us anything on the surface to indicate that they were having any problems whatsoever. They always acted like they were hot to trot and that they were ready to get laid.

What they were doing was playing mind games with us. And I don't do mind games.

And, being secretive is okay, it's fine, but a little information is good to know. One night, she said to me,

'After the first time we did it, I cried for days and wouldn't let him touch me for months afterwards. I couldn't even look at him.'

But that's all she said and when I asked why, she just shrugged and changed the subject.

That should have been a sign, but we were pretty naïve about all this and just felt sorry for her. And the reason we felt sorry for her? Every time we were with them, she told us some sad story about her life. I won't repeat any of them but these stories would go on and on and anytime the conversation would fall in my lap, she'd have to snatch it back with another one of her sad stories. I didn't want to seem like a bitch, so I let it go. But she couldn't stand not being the center of attention. And when I'd point this out to my husband, he'd say, 'Well, good grief, that was a bad story. It's horrible to think of something like that happening to someone.'

So, I'd let it go. Like I said, I didn't want to look like a bitch and I'm not that jealous to begin with. It wasn't that big a deal.

Well, come to find out, she was just insecure and pretended to be this sexually liberated person that she wasn't. She couldn't handle swinging and the idea of her husband being with another woman (me!) was killing her. It was downright killing her. And to top it off, after a while, he stopped being able to get an erection for me and that made me doubt myself. Even though I know women don't have anything to do with it, it made me feel so ugly and undesirable. And she was always fucking my husband and getting off, though I think she faked most of her orgasms. My husband said she never moved during sex, only laid there.

After about a month, I'd had enough and wanted out. We fought over it cause my husband was sure things would work out and finding people to swing with is so hard. I kept doing it even though I knew something was wrong. I knew something wasn't right about this picture.

And again, they were playing these mind games. They kept telling us we were such good friends and they were so happy they'd met us and we were cool people and all this shit. And I felt bad because I really didn't feel the same way about them! But by them doing this, it really clouded things up. My husband got one message—they wanted us to be friends—and I got another—they were overcompensating for something. I thought it might be that the husband couldn't get hard for me and that's why they said the nice things. But I didn't *feel* like they meant them.

And, of course, this caused us to fight. And we got into some major fights about it, to say the least.

Why didn't we stop right then and there? I don't know why! It was weird. It was almost like we had made a commitment to *make this thing work.* And it was never going to work! Maybe we were caught up in a vicious cycle. I don't know. It was hell. I guess the signs were there, but we didn't see them. We kept thinking it would get better and we didn't know enough about swinging to know when to move on. Maybe you just get caught up in this vicious cycle and can't get out of it. We were caught up in something, God only knows what.

We wanted to get along with them and because they portrayed this image of being sexually free, we thought they were fine with swinging. He might have been, but she certainly wasn't.

Another thing was *they* kept on insisting they were cool as shit about swinging and we, again being naïve, went along with it. Even though I brought up things here and there to let them know we were cool with *not* having sex, they would insist on having sex *every* time we saw them. And because the guy couldn't get a hard-on, she and my husband were the only ones actually having sex. I once told him, 'It's like we're seeing them so you and her can have a fuck date!' And the reason he couldn't get hard for me? She'd tear him a new one if he did.

Of course, this made him feel bad and he kept promising to make it up to me, but it never turned out right.

Well, needless to say, it all came to a head one night. The girl just freaked out on us. She broke down and cried and basically fell apart, telling us we were ruining her marriage and all this stuff that made us feel like one-hundred percent shit.

We left feeling really, really bad. Like we were bad people for putting them through that.

That's where it ended with them. But it took a while for my husband and I to get our relationship straightened out. We started fighting because of all this guilt we felt for being such 'bad' people. It nearly tore us apart. I accused him of caring more for them because I wanted to end it months before it ended. He fought back, even though he knew I was right. I mean, obviously he didn't care more for them than he did me, it's just that he knew I was right way back when to call it off.

He also fought back because he knew how much pain I was feeling and he felt guilty for helping to cause that pain because he hadn't agreed to call it off. He was projecting onto me. We went in circles for months, this thing eating us from the inside out.

I love my husband more than anything but I actually considered leaving him.

Well, we finally got over it. It took a lot of healing and love, but we weathered it. And we're cool now. In fact, we're better than ever, it's actually made us a stronger couple.

I'm just glad we stuck together. We gave swinging another shot. We really enjoy it. But anytime I think of that couple, I get a sick feeling. I know I can never make what happened 'right' and I feel bad that I can't. I don't have any hard feelings anymore but if they'd just been honest with themselves and other with people, all of this could have been avoided."

Before I heard this story, I thought I'd heard everything. I guess I hadn't.

Swinging can be emotionally damaging. We can ascertain that from this sad story. You're looking for a reason to feel bad because of all the guilt you feel. You might even look for a reason to feel bad because of all the *good* feeling swinging has given you. The mind works in mysterious ways. Sometimes we want to punish ourselves for no other reason than we think we *should.* Other people will not only do it to you, but you will do it to yourself.

Note: *Don't let it drive you crazy.*

As I've said, if you're not suited, *DO NOT* put anyone through this sort of thing. Don't be selfish. Just don't do it. Please.

Too close for comfort.

You might find yourself in a situation where another couple, or only one member of that couple, is contacting you a little too much. In fact, they have become pests. You've been nice to them to the point that they're driving you crazy. They're needy and have to have lots of attention.

Chances are, they don't realize they're doing it. They might think you're better friends than you are. You, on the other hand, are ready to cut the ties. Maybe you weren't sexually compatible with them or maybe you just didn't click. So how do you get out of it without looking like an asshole?

Good luck. Most times, it's hard to break ties without some hurt feelings. There are people out there who need so much from others that they don't really care what they have to do (or how they look) to get it. Maybe they think if they pester you enough, you'll break down and do what they want.

My advice is to be polite, send them a nice email and tell them you're taking a break right now. I don't see any reason to hurt their feelings if it's not necessary. If they don't take the hint, (most likely they won't) then sometimes you have to be an asshole. Don't return their emails. The fact of the matter is some people just don't take hints. You have to be rude to get them out of your life. You can waste a lot of time trying to be nice.

Personal experience:
Not too long ago, I was contacted by a single guy who wanted to exchange emails. Keep in mind he was a *married* single guy and his wife didn't know anything about all this. I

felt bad for him and thought I should be nice. (I sometimes think that a lot of trouble is caused in the world because of our inability to not be nice.) He would email sometimes four and five times a day. At first, it was fine and even a little fun to have so much attention. I responded to his emails. Why not?

Then he wanted to get personal. Too personal. He asked me questions like, "Where do you live?" (I don't tell strangers where I live.) I would tell him it was none of his business. He'd tell me he was dying to meet me. I would say, "We can be friends but that's it. I don't get involved with men whose wives don't know what they're doing."

After a while, I'd dread opening my mailbox because I knew there would be a ton of emails from him. I stopped responding and he would send emails saying that he knew he was a pest but he really liked me and wanted to meet me. It was bordering on creepy.

I put him straight and told him nothing would ever happen. Before long, I just started deleting his emails when I got them. He got the hint and has since stopped emailing me. Perhaps this was a little harsh, but it was all I could do to send the message out that I wasn't interested. And that I don't have that much time in the day to respond to four or five emails from the same person.

If it's just one member of the couple just contacting you, listen to this: *Don't go there! It will only cause you pain. You* are asking for nothing but trouble.

Related experience:
This is from Joe.

"They were a great couple and we spent a lot of time in the hot tub with them drinking beers and having sex. When she called me out of the blue, I didn't think anything of it. I thought she was calling to set up a date for Saturday or something. It never occurred to me to ask her how she'd gotten my work number; I just figured my wife had given it to her. When I told my wife about, she kind of flipped out.

'No, I did not give her your number. Why would I do that?'

Well, that's where it ended. She called me the very next day and suggested that just she and I meet. Alone. I flat-out told her no. She got really pissed off at me and told me it wouldn't mean anything and that no one would have to know. Well, maybe, but I love my wife and kids and that was one risk I wasn't about to take."

As I've said, there are risks involved. Other people can develop feelings for you or for your partner. If this happens, break it off. You are not only at risk for hurting them, but you are at risk of hurting yourself. And people can be malicious.

What if it's you that has feelings? First of all, know that it's human to have feelings for other people and sometimes it doesn't mean anything. Ask yourself exactly what you are feeling. Is it really love? Or is it just a crush? Remember, they may not feel the same way about *you*. Are you willing to risk your homelife and your relationship on the off-chance of getting together with this other person? Think about the people you could potentially hurt. Yourself being one of them. Besides you're already screwing them, what else are you looking for?

Just don't make a fool of yourself. If it's really love, then my suggestion is to wait and see what happens. If he/she feels the same way, they may come to you. If you go to them and start something, expect the shit to hit the fan. Be prepared for a big mess. But if it's not love, the feelings will pass and you'll be glad you didn't make a fool of yourself.

Impotence. It *can* happen to everyone.

You're all excited about your next date or party and when you get there, you realize you are going to have no trouble hooking up with the person/couple you desire. You find a secluded corner and after a few minutes of intense foreplay, you realize your new lover isn't hard. Or, if you are the new lover, you realize your fella isn't responding like he should. In fact, he was hard but he stopped working at the point of insertion. What can you do?

First of all, *DO NOT FREAK OUT!*

It has nothing to do with how desirable you are. In fact, it has nothing to do with you and if you're a male reading this, there is nothing wrong with you.

So what went wrong?

Many things. Too much alcohol. You maybe have been too excited, and, yes, you can be too excited. Performance anxiety. There might also be an audience watching you. Or if you're doing a same room swap, just knowing there's another guy in the room can do it. Many things come into play here. Swinging is an intense experience, especially in a group setting. It can overwhelm a person to the extent that they, simply, can't do what comes naturally. Especially if you're new to the Lifestyle.

Don't obsess that it's not working! This will only make it not work more! Take a break. Breathe. Talk about anything but the impotence. Take the attention away from it and after a few minutes, try again.

Getting or receiving head during this time usually does the trick. A nice, good stroke is always good, as well. Go to a more secluded spot away from other people. And try, try again.

Personal experience:

I hooked up with this guy once who was beyond gorgeous. As my friends would say, he was one fine piece of ass. We talked and teased and flirted on and off all night.

We finally found ourselves alone in the bathroom and we started at it. He was an excellent kisser and I love being kissed. After we kissed for a little while, I wanted to get to it.

I put my hand on his dick and he was ready! Good for me, good for him. I gave him a little head then we decided it was time to have sex.

He got in and everything was fine. A-OK. But then, he...to put it nicely, deflated. I could feel it, too. I was a little crushed, thinking he really didn't desire me and I let all those feminine insecurities get the best of me. *I was such a loser!*

He said, "I'm sorry. It's not you."

I looked at him and could tell he was. Sorry, that is.

"Let me see what I can do," I told him.

I got down on my knees and got to work on him. I went at it for a good five minutes but nothing happened. Well, he'd go through stages of being hard, then of not being hard.

Then he told me, "I'm really drunk. I don't think I can do it."

Well, now that made sense.

After we had a good laugh, we gave each other a hug and promised to try again once he dried out. It took a little while and I was getting ready to leave when he waved me down.

Yup. He was ready. I took him back into the bathroom. You can guess what happened next.

Ladies, if your guy can't get it up, simply shrug it off and go find yourself a girl. Or another guy.

It can happen to everyone and it happens more than you think. You have to realize that this is a sort of unusual situation for sex. I wouldn't go as far to call it abnormal, but it *is* atypical. It's not everyday you have sex with so many people around. And have sex with an almost stranger.

If you're a guy reading this and you find yourself in a situation where it's just not happening, please don't expect the girl to stand around all night trying to get you hard. Allow her to do her thing for ten or so minutes then let her off the hook. Okay? You'll do better next time.

Swinging rule #3.

Swinging is a very private thing between you and your partner and not between you and the rest of the world.

When your friends become suspicious.

After you've started swinging, you might notice something different about the people around you. They're acting a little abnormally. A little *unusual*. They're eying you a little...*suspiciously*. One of them may even have the nerve to ask, "Where were you last weekend? I called and you weren't around." There may be accusation in their voice. Maybe a little hurt. And that's because they've become suspicious *of you.*

It's like this. One weekend you're sitting around at home with nothing to do. The next, you're getting a sitter and going to a party at the home of somebody whom none of your friends have ever met or heard about.

Suddenly, you've got all these new friends. *Where the hell did these people come from?* Suddenly, you're going out of town at least once a month. *Why?* You're acting a little suspicious. *Have you noticed that Carol always avoids questions about she did over the weekend?* More than likely, you've also started turning down invites to be with your straight friends. *They never have time for me anymore. Are they mad about something? Did I do something?* Suddenly, you're acting a lot cooler and this makes others wonder, *What's up with them?* You've become the object of suspicion. You're acting odd, unusual. You're giggling more. You grin a lot. You've lost weight. You are looking really,

really sexy, too. Something is definitely going on and the people around you want to know the score.

You don't really want to tell them, do you? Well, I don't.

I wouldn't suggest it for you either. Some of my friends are the most open-minded people you could ever hope to meet. But I like to keep them separate from my swinging friends. There is a small chance they won't understand. And they're good friends and I don't want to lose them.

But why do they get suspicious?

People are naturally curious, not to mention naturally suspicious. We've all been trained to ask questions about the people we care about. This is all well and good, but sometimes, people go beyond being curious and get downright nosey. They seem to think you've got something "going on" and they want to know who, what, when and where.

Personal experience:

Just after we got back from Hedonism III, our friend, let's call him Jake, began to ask a lot of questions. One of the main being, "Did you go to the Decadent Hotel down there? Some guy at work told me they have this place called the Decadent Hotel and people walk around naked and have sex everywhere."

Of course, we hadn't been to the Decadent Hotel, as it doesn't exist, but we *had* been to Hedonism and people do walk around naked and have sex everywhere. We knew he was trying to trip us up by switching the names around.

We knew he wanted us to say, "It's not the Decadent Hotel! It's Hedonism and it's *cool.*" And then the cat would have been out of the bag. And more than likely, he wanted us to confess because he was suspicious. He wanted to know what we'd been doing.

Wasn't going to happen.

What did we do? We told him no such place existed and kept having him repeat the name of the so-called naked resort until we wore him out and he gave up.

Related experience:

Amber and I got a good laugh out of this one.

"We were so stupid. We met this great couple and were having so much fun with them that we started to invite them to our regular parties and really integrated them into our normal lives. Like I said, they were that great and we really wanted everyone to meet them because they were so great. We even invited them to a comedy club with some of our family members. Stupid!

I guess we felt it was normal, swinging, I mean. Since we didn't have a problem with it, why should anyone else? So why hide these great people we'd met just because someone else might not approve?

Okay, so we had this party and had about twenty or so of our non-swinging friends along with the couple. It was fun. I was in the kitchen and my friend James came into the room to help me mix some drinks.

He said something about how good the party was and I said, 'It is good, isn't it?'

He stared at me for a long moment and said, 'It's also good to see you invited your swinger friends.'

I nearly choked. I shook my head and started to explain, 'Swinger friends? What do you mean? What's that? I've never heard of such a thing! I used to work with her and she emailed the other day and I just thought I'd be nice and invite them since they don't know that many people in town.'

He gave me a *very* odd look and said, 'I was just joking, Amber. Geez. Lighten up.'

We came *this* close to getting busted. From there on out, we kept our two worlds separate."

People are smart. They can and will figure stuff out. My suggestion to you is to keep it separate as Amber learned. But know that people will ask questions. Be prepared to answer them beforehand. Have your excuses ready. Don't offer additional explanations for your behavior. You're an adult and it is your right to do as you please! And if people get too nosy, tell them it's none of their business. Because it isn't.

When a club gets busted.

There were people all around. Some in secluded areas. Some out in the open. They were doing what comes naturally, fucking and having a great time. Then, all a sudden, cops burst in and bust the place.

Unfortunately, this is not unheard of in the swinging community. Clubs and/or swing parties sometimes do get busted by the police.

Related experience:

I checked my email to find a message from one of my swinger buddies. It read: "Did you hear about the club? They got busted!" She had attached a link, so I hit it and read the report.

Basically what happened was that the police had been tipped off about this club, which was an on-premise club. There was some pretty wild stuff going on (gangbangs, etc.). They arrested over one-hundred people and a lot of lives were in chaos for a while.

The reason? The club didn't have a liquor license. The owners were serving liquor and thought that since they required a membership fee before anyone could go in, they were legal. They thought they had private club status. Well, they didn't and the cops were able to bust them on a technicality.

The liquor thing gave the cops a reason to come in. And then they arrested people for indecent exposure and stuff like that. All charges were later dropped but not before all these people's names had been printed in the newspaper and they were thoroughly embarrassed.

Even though it's unusual for this to happen, it *does* happen. Depending on the area you live in. Technically, it's not against the law, though some places do have laws against anal sex, fellatio, adultery, etc. (You have to keep in mind that these laws were written a long time ago. It is my opinion that they should be updated.)

The point is that cops *can* find a reason to bust a club, as they did in the example above. However, one of the most common reasons cops show up at a swing party/club is because someone called them.

But why would someone "tip" off the cops? The reasons are very simple. A person might have been to the club beforehand and gotten rejected. (Boo fucking hoo!) They might have gotten jealous about something their lover did. (Cry me a river…) They might just be a mean spirited person who wants others to suffer for no other reason than they have the power to do something like that.

It can also happen in a domestic situation. I know one couple whose neighbor called the cops on them whenever they'd have people over. They finally gave up giving parties because it became such a hassle.

She told me, "I just couldn't do it anymore. I mean, every single time I'd have a party, I'd get a visit from some cop! I mean, come on! Don't they have lives of their own? Why are they always watching mine?!"

Might be because they were having so much fun at their parties and some people just don't want that, do they? Some people want you to be just as miserable as they are. And with the law on their side, they can make it happen by just picking up the phone and claiming "The music is too loud," or "Cars are blocking driveways," or "I think I saw a naked person in their back yard!"

It doesn't really matter what excuse they come up with, it *always* seems to work.

Related experience:

This comes from Martin.

"I hosted a party once a month at my place for over six years. Six years and not one single incident! We always had a good time and that's why I had the parties. I enjoy seeing people enjoying themselves. Things could get pretty wild. Women were always naked and the men...well most of them just sat back and watched.

Well, one night it happened. It was bound to. A good thing can't last, can it? There was a couple there and they started arguing. Seems as though his woman gave some guy a blowjob and he couldn't handle it. I mean, for God's sake, what did he think was going to happen at a swing party? She was ready to party and he obviously wasn't.

I got up and told them to please leave because they were disturbing everyone else. No one likes to see that at a swing party. It makes you start thinking maybe there is something wrong with it to bring out such strong emotions.

He grabbed his woman's hand and pulled her out of the house and I thought it was over. The party got started again and everyone started having a good time. We forgot about them.

Well, not for long. A little while later, two cop cars came crawling up the drive and I just knew the son of a bitch had ratted on us. He had. It was a mess. People were running for cover, trying to find their clothes. The cops handcuffed a few and read them their rights. For what? Having sex? Since when is *that* against the fucking law? They couldn't get me on anything because I don't charge a fee. They mentioned something about creating a disturbance. But that didn't hold any water because my place is well off the beaten path. My closest neighbor is a mile or two away. They tried and failed to get me. But it still ruined my parties because people were afraid to come to them. I hope that guy is happy. If I ever see him again…well, let's just say it won't be pretty."

This is just a warning. Please do not let it deter you from enjoying the Lifestyle. Just be informed that things like this can happen. Keep an eye out for freaky stuff happening i.e. couples arguing, somebody storming out, two guys throwing punches. If this happens, it might be your clue to get lost.

Hedonism. Yea or nay?

Yea, of course!

There are two Hedonisms, II and III. They are all-inclusive (everything included in one price) resorts located in beautiful Jamaica.

Just a few things about Hedonism. The locals call it the "Zoo" (you can probably guess why), each resort has clothing and nude beaches and pools. And they make a killer mud slide.

Once you arrive, you will notice at first that there are naked people walking around everywhere. You can even see them in the buffet area. (I believe that dress is required for the reservations-only restaurants.)

Most people who go to Hedo are very laid back and nice. It's a good place to hook up with someone because there are plenty of areas conducive to having sex. You will more than likely see people getting it on. I saw a man get what looked like a very good blowjob late one night in the hot tub.

Most rooms come with a Jacuzzi and a small refrigerator. The beds are king sized. But who cares what the rooms look like? If you go to Hedo, the last thing on your mind will be how nice your room is. You won't be spending that much time in it.

Some fun stuff to do there is, of course, nude sun bathing, playing nude pool volleyball and participating in one of the many "naughty" games the Hedo staff set up. Prizes are sometimes involved. There is also a disco and a piano bar. You can also do snorkeling and scuba diving if you like.

They have so much fun stuff to do there, it's hard to list it all. Go and find out for yourself.

Personal experience:
During our second day at Hedo, we decided to do the Dunn's River Falls trip. It's a breathtaking waterfall that you climb up with a bunch of other people. You walk up hand and in, boy girl/boy girl. My husband fell and busted his ass on a rock when a large woman lost her balance and pulled him down. (You should have seen the look on his face!)

Well, on the way over, there were a few couples on the bus. Most everyone made small talk. One couple in particular began to talk to us. After a few minutes of mindless chitchat about the buffet and the beach and the snorkeling, the wife exclaimed, "And I didn't even know there were naked people here! I thought it was a regular resort! I was like, *what did I get myself into?*"

The husband added, "Yeah, we went to the pool and everyone was naked."

My husband and I exchanged looks. We might have been some of those naked people they saw. However, we couldn't believe they didn't know what Hedo was all about. But we let it go. I mean, whatever...

"Oh," we said and changed the subject.

Well, after we returned from the trip, we went straight to the nude pool. And there was that couple, both naked as jailbirds! And, of course, they pretended not to know who we were. We returned the favor.

Hedonism is somewhat expensive, but not anymore than some of the nicer "regular" resorts. It's worth every dime, though. So start saving your money if you're going to be a swinger. You are going to have a blast there.

And, no Hedonism did not pay for this endorsement.

Has Hollywood ruined sex?

We're about to the end now and I wanted to include this last bit of information that I feel is pertinent to the book. And the reason I want to include it is because a lot of people out there have morality issues with extramarital sex and/or swinging. Religion aside, I believe one of the reasons is because of all the bullshit movies we watch.

Hear me out.

We all have this stupid storybook notion of living happily ever after. Where did we get it? We got it from movies like *Pretty Woman, When Harry Met Sally* and all those other boring chick flicks that make us feel bad about ourselves because we don't have this picture perfect storybook romantic life.

These movies make us feel bad about ourselves because they put out a standard that's impossible to live up to. No hooker has had a rich john rescue her. No two friends have taken *that* long to get together. People don't meet from miles away at the top of the Empire State building. They meet at the bar down the street. Or at the grocery store or some other typical place.

So, yes, in my honest opinion, Hollywood has ruined sex to a certain extent. Movies just aren't all that realistic and, while appearing to be realistic on the surface, it's the details that get fuzzy. We know things don't work out like they do in the movies. These things *could* happen but usually they just don't.

First, we all know that, as adults, if you have really good sex you look like shit afterwards. (Though very sexy in an animalistic kind of way. *Mmmm...*) Your hair is going in all directions, you have big red blotches all over your body from the oh, so delicious rubbing and you're usually panting. You might even, if you're lucky, be a little sticky.

In the movies, lovers look like they just stepped out of a beauty parlor. That is if you even see sex in movies, which most times, you just don't. Now you get the soft fade. If you want to watch sex, you have to rent a porno. (Or go to a swing club.)

Hollywood has also put this ridiculous moral code in their movies. They don't make many movies about swinging. Sure, you can find the occasional documentary about swinging, but that's about it. Swinging is a huge part of our society, and as underground and as hush-hush as it is, it is a permanent fixture. But people don't talk about it. Maybe if you don't talk about it, it's really not there.

The most typical example of a movie about swinging is *Bob, Ted, Carol and Alice,* which is about thirty some odd years old. In it, the characters try for a good old fashioned wife swap. But, of course, in the end, the characters just couldn't go through with it. They just lay there in a big bed and looked very uncomfortable.

Real swingers wouldn't have started in the bed. They would have ended up in the bed, exhausted.

Affairs are looked upon not as a learning/growing experience but as a tragic event. It's worse than murder. *How could they do this?!* World's crash down, people (usually women) weep. Families are split up. All this havoc is wreaked because someone had sex with someone besides their partner.

If this were the way it really happened in real life, most everyone would be divorced. They don't seem to understand, most of us don't have time to have these extreme nervous breakdowns because someone cheated. We have to work and feed our families and pay our bills.

So I ask this: *When did the public ask Hollywood to tell us all how to live?*

In the movies, a kiss is referred to as the ultimate intimacy. *The ultimate intimacy?* That's a joke. If you want to get down and dirty, the ultimate intimacy is having someone's penis in me. *That's* intimacy. Kissing, to me at least, is just a way to say hello before you get down to business. It's nice. It's wonderful. But it is in no way the end-all-be-all of intimacy.

Maybe kissing is a big deal because that's all they can show in movies now. To them, it *might* be the ultimate intimacy.

Hollywood also fosters the notion of there being only one person for every person. Do you realize how many people there are in the world and that this incredibly preposterous idea goes against our very nature? When we were living in caves, women *had* to sleep with a lot of men in order to survive. Men *had* to sleep with a lot of women in order to ensure at least one child would make it so their genes would continue into the next generation. It was not a lifestyle choice back then, it was a survival technique.

There can be a *one* but that doesn't mean you can't have sex with people who aren't *The One.* A lot of people believe in soul mates and there's nothing wrong with that. Just understand that having sex with someone other than the soul mate doesn't diminish the relationship.

Another thing is that Hollywood has this idea that once you're married, you're pretty much dead. There are all these wacky movies about two people trying to hook up with the "right one". The one that got away or the one they just met that is about to get married and get away. They go through idiotic mishap after idiotic mishap before they finally land "the one." Then they live happily ever after. What I've always been interested in is what happens *after* they get together. Do they disappear from the earth? I've always longed to see real movies about real people after the storybook wedding. I've always wanted to see if other people have the same problems I have had.

Not gonna happen.

This whole notion of *The One* is a fallacy. It's also pretty dim. Most swingers laugh at this notion. After I married the person I loved more than anything, I'd never felt so alive. It was only in later years that I had the desire to go outside the marital bounds and be a person who explored her desires. I thank God I have a man who is as open-minded as I am and allows me the freedom I need.

How many movies do you watch a month? Yes, it's a great pastime, but their hypocritical views on relationships and sex can get into your head and make you doubt yourself. Movies and television are a main force in our culture. In fact, unfortunately, it's about the only culture we have. So the more you watch, the more likely you are going to be influenced. You just have to recognize the signs and learn how to roll your eyes.

The point of all this discussion is for you to understand that swinging is a personal choice but because of our culture, Hollywood in particular, it is looked upon as being wrong. *Remember, this is just some else's opinion.* And it is a wrong and misleading opinion.

Besides, do you actually think the people who make these movies actually follow the advice dealt out by them? Just read the tabloids and make your own conclusions.

Sex is just sex. The same kind of sex our caveman ancestors had. Sex is not love or candy. Sex is not security. Sex is not a romantic Hollywood movie. It is, pure and simple, fucking.

If all else fails…

You've tried it. You've went to the parties, to the clubs, you've met couples and went on dates. And it's just not happening. You either find yourself pulling back or others pulling back from you.

Don't take it personally. Don't beat yourself up over it. It's no big deal. You can give it a little more time if you like. You never know who might be around the corner.

Sometimes, the *idea* of doing it is just as good as the act itself. Knowing that you can do it, knowing your relationship won't fall apart if you have sex with someone else may be all you need.

I suggest you pat yourself and your lover on the back for being such open-minded people. No. Make love to them instead and know that even if it didn't work out, you still have each other. And knowing you are with such a fantastic person should give you reason to rejoice.

You're a cool person for at least trying and no one can ever take that away from you.

It all worked out.

Three cheers for the open-minded couple! Hip! Hip! Hooray! Hip! Hip! Hooray!

You did it all. You forced yourself into that intimidating looking swing club and partied your ass off. You met a great couple and you fucked their brains out, then you went home and fucked your lover's brains out, too. You sashayed into that swing party and you had sex with strangers. *YOU HAD SEX WITH STRANGERS!* Or maybe you just kissed them and left them panting for more. You peeped in glory holes. Maybe you *participated* in glory holes. *Good Lord! What would your mother think?!* (Who cares? Don't let her find out.) You danced nude in a roomful of watchful eyes and *it didn't bother you.* You had sex with people whose names you didn't bother to find out! You naughty thing! You met a couple who had issues and you were smart enough to recognize them and smart enough to back away. You fought that old green-eyed monster and kicked his ass and sent him away for good.

You are one helluva person. Anyone ever tell you that?

But most importantly, you went home and fell asleep in your lover's arms and were glad to be there. And you know that while having sex with other people is wonderful and great, it could never compare to sex with your lover, who lies in your arms feeling the same way about you.

Is there anything better in life? Who needs drugs when you've got swinging? Who would bother with an affair when you've got swinging? Why would anyone be so stupid to lie and cheat in this world when you've got swinging?

So, is there anything better than swinging? Well, if there is, you better let me know because I want to experience it, too.

CPSIA information can be obtained at www.ICGtesting.com
Printed in the USA
266977BV00003B/2/A